TOTAL
SELLING

A Step-by-Step Guide
to Successful Sales

WARREN WECHSLER

SOURCEBOOKS, INC.
NAPERVILLE, ILLINOIS

All names used in "Sales Doctor" segments have been changed.

Published by Sourcebooks, Inc.
P.O. Box 4410, Naperville, Illinois 60567-4410
(630) 961-3900
FAX: (630) 961-2168
www.sourcebooks.com
Library of Congress Cataloging-in-Publication Data

Library of Congress Cataloging-in-Publication Data

Wechsler, Warren.
  Total selling : a step-by-step guide to successful sales / by Warren Wechsler.
    p. cm.
  ISBN 1-4022-0294-6 (alk. paper)
  1. Sales Management. 2. Selling. I. Title.
HF5438.4.W424 2004
658.85—dc22

                              2004013910

Printed and bound in the United States of America
VP 10 9 8 7 6 5 4 3 2 1

Acknowledgments

Many thanks to many people. To my wife, Gail for continuing to live a life of high standards and inspiring me to raise the bar. To my children, Alison and Samantha, for their enthusiastic support and a natural curiosity to question my ideas when they see and hear me in action. To my associate, Susan Korsgaden, for all the details and hours of transcribing and clearing the path for me. To my agent, Jöelle Delbourgo, for having the vision and knowing what this book was going to be even before I did. To my editor, Hillel Black at Sourcebooks, for editing expertise and gentle guidance. To Dean Draznin and Jeffrey Hedquist, who counsel with me to pursue excellence and expect the best of each other. Many others who have helped me, while unmentioned, are thanked in my heart.

"The thrill is not just in winning, but in the courage to join the race."—Anonymous

Chapter One

Becoming a Total Salesperson

Introduction

Total Selling is a comprehensive guide for salespeople, entrepreneurs, and business professionals. The concepts are based on timeless principles. The content is professional, practical, and based on common sense. Total Selling is field-tested by my long career as a salesperson, sales manager, and sales educator. Total Selling is not manipulative or fad-based. Rather, *Total Selling* introduces three powerful, connected, and complete concepts—process, planning, and practice—that create a proven, winning formula for selling excellence.

Success Speaks for Itself

I've been a sales professional for more than twenty-five years, as a salesperson, sales manager, and business owner. Over the years, I've seen an incredible amount of misguided and useless information on professional selling techniques. I've also been privileged to know some of the most successful educators and leaders in the sales industry—people who have satisfying, meaningful, and useful selling ideas. The principles and techniques you are about to learn have been field-tested by those and thousands of others who have attended my seminars or worked with me one-on-one or through my consulting work within their organization.

Early in my career, I began to understand the basic principles of selling, and my sales began to grow. In fact, they doubled in one year. As my sales grew, my confidence grew. I was soon promoted to sales management positions where I had the opportunity to help others get off on the right foot in their selling careers. When I started to teach others this profession, I found myself remembering my own successes and failures and thought that the best way to share my knowledge would be to have people read books, attend seminars, and listen to audio cassettes on the topics of selling that had helped me. It occurred to me that I had picked up lots of ideas from many different sources, yet there was not one book, tape, or seminar that told me the whole story.

Eventually, I wrote down the principles of success that I had learned, used, and developed and created a blueprint for success. Knowing that in any field of endeavor, a step-by-step approach built on a strong foundation would yield the best results, I developed a model that would be simple to understand, easy to follow, and based on common sense.

Since then, I've had clients, seminar participants, and almost every sales manager and sales executive I've come across ask how to create a complete selling system for their business. They want to know how to be strategic in their thinking and how to find and develop the tools and systems to put their selling and business skills into practice. That's how *Total Selling* came to be. It combines the best strategy I know of for finding, winning, and keeping customers.

Building a successful business isn't for the feeble-hearted. There are numerous stops and starts, and the path can be a minefield of obstacles, rejection, and failure. But if you are willing to learn the principles and techniques I'm offering in this book, mastering Total Selling will be a matter of course.

Overcoming Difficult Times

I understand what salespeople are experiencing today. In 1991, in a matter of six weeks, my two best clients were acquired by other companies. Overnight, my company's revenue was reduced by 60 percent. This loss would be a devastating blow to many businesses, yet utilizing the principles of Total Selling, I was able to rebuild my revenue to previous levels in less than ninety days.

The principles of Total Selling passed their greatest test in the wake of the catastrophic events of September 11, 2001. By the end of the day on September 12, 2001, all of Total Selling, Inc.'s business for September and October that included airline travel (over 75 percent of total revenue) had been canceled. Despite this dire situation, I possessed a clear understanding of what to do based on the knowledge of Total Selling: develop a sales plan, follow a step-by-step sales process, and utilize effective sales practices. By the first quarter of 2002, my business was booming. Revenue had exceeded pre–September 11 levels. This continued throughout 2002. In fact, the year 2002 was the company's best year, which serves to demonstrate the power of Total Selling.

Many books have been written that touch on various aspects of the content in *Total Selling*. This is the only book that has the total package. It is the comprehensive guide that presents the tools, principles, and techniques for any salesperson, business owner or other professional to be a total salesperson.

Read the newspaper. Listen to the radio. Watch television. Browse the Internet. It is easy to be overwhelmed by the negative messages that we hear and see. At any given time, wars are raging on several continents. There are ethnic and religious disputes in many regions. Catastrophic natural events even have their own channel on cable—The Weather Channel! And there's always plenty of bad economic news to report. Unemployment is the measuring stick. It's never "95 percent employment this month." It's always "5 percent are out of work." You get the idea. Negative news is what sells newspapers. Even within our own businesses, the messages are oftentimes negative. We talk about lost accounts instead of won accounts. We come back to the office and discuss the two things that went wrong in our day in terms of service breakdowns or product outages, and forget that ninety-eight things went well that day. And as salespeople, more than most people, we have a responsibility to control what we control and be positive. That is what a total salesperson does. Now is the best time for salespeople to think positive and move forward resolutely. *Total Selling* inspires salespeople and businesspeople to take action. It's simple. It's all spelled out. And anybody can learn to do it.

In the first section of the book, you will learn about the three major concepts of Total Selling. Process is explained first. To be successful in sales, we need to have a clear understanding of what a sales process is and how to create one. You will learn a step-by-step, definable, repeatable, and measurable sales process. The second aspect of Total Selling is having a sales plan. Developing a sound sales plan is what we do to make sure that we are doing the right things everyday in our business. Many times, we confuse being busy with being successful. When we have an effective sales plan, it becomes very easy for us to look at what we do every day and compare it to what we know will ensure our success. The third idea is called sales practice. If having a sales plan is doing the right thing, then sales practice is doing things right. Sales practice enables us to make sure that we are squeezing every ounce of productivity out of every work day.

Throughout this book, the three major principles are discussed in great detail. These elements are equally important. In fact, you might think that mastering any one of these concepts would be enough to help you be successful in your sales career. Nothing is further than the truth. It's like a three-legged stool. If two legs are strong and one leg is not functioning, what would happen if you put a glass of water on it? Obviously, the water would spill and the glass would fall to the floor and break. It is absolutely imperative for us to master all three principles.

Total Selling Explained

Let's look at the experiences of three salespeople.

Rob had a plan. He intended to be one of the top ten salespeople in his company. He knew exactly how much business he needed to write. He utilized good sales practices, as he wrote all his action items in his personal planner and he recorded every interaction with his prospects in great detail in his daily diary. Yet he didn't achieve his goals because he didn't know who his best prospects were, how many prospects he needed, and what to say on the initial approach. Rob was missing a key component for sales excellence. Once he understood and mastered an effective sales *process*, he rocketed to the top ten in six months.

Catherine had more ambition, made more calls, and had seven times more accounts than any other salesperson in her organization. She was also below average in sales revenue and income. Why? Because Catherine had no idea what the big picture was. She mistook busy work and any activity with proper and prioritized actions. After learning and integrating the components of a sound sales *plan* into her selling career, Catherine stopped calling on two-thirds of her accounts, worked less, earned more, and had more fun.

Alan was always a day late and a dollar short. Although he had a model sales plan and could define down to the finest detail what his sales process looked like, he was a failure. When asked who he was going to call today, what he and his clients discussed last time, and what the next steps were, he was clueless. He was so frustrated that he was about to leave his profession after ten years and start all over again doing something else. After he learned how to apply best sales *practices* to become a superior self-manager, however, Alan became a leader in his company, sought out by others for guidance and counsel. Fifteen years later, he is the number one salesperson in his office and has realized all of his dreams.

The Three Ps

I have a confession to make. I was trained by the "go get 'em" model. I was hired by a terrific company with a great reputation, wonderful products and services, and hundreds of salespeople. One day after eighteen months in the "sales training" program, I had spent weeks to months in accounting, finance, manufacturing, distribution, store services, catalog, marketing, etc., etc., etc. Every aspect of the business, except sales. I was approached by the vice president of sales one day. He called me into his office and, with great enthusiasm, told me that I was ready to graduate from the sales trainee program and would be assigned a sales territory. And here came my sales education: "Warren, go get 'em!"

It didn't work for me and it won't work for you. "Go get 'em" is not a sales process.

What makes a champion selling superstar? In my view there are three absolute, nonnegotiable, paramount principles that we must follow in order to be champions in selling: process, plan, and practice. In order to be a champion in sales, we have to understand and use the three P's. We have to have a sales process. We have to be prepared. And we have to practice our craft. It's simple, definable, and repeatable—and anyone can learn how to do it.

Process Sales process means that we have a system in place by which we run our sales business. Many people are trained in sales using that "go get 'em" model. Well, "Go get 'em" doesn't work. You have to have a process. You have to have an understanding of how you're going to implement a selling system.

Let's look at how mastering a process is involved in some other areas of life. Let's begin with golf. The process begins with driving.

You have to get the ball off the tee.

Then you're onto the fairway. You have to understand how to get the ball down the fairway. And you need to master the short game, putting. Those are the three ideas involved in golf.

Of course, there are sand wedges, blasting out of traps, getting out of water, and all that. But the fundamentals are driving, short game, and putting.

How about my specialty, long-distance running? The process is to run a long, slow distance as a base, hill work to build your stamina and strength, and speed work to enhance your leg turnover so you can run fast for a long amount of time.

What about selling? Is there a process in selling? Should we just wing it? Should we wait for the phone to ring? Of course not.

In order to be successful in sales, you have to have an explicit process in mind. You're going to learn such a process as you become a Total Salesperson.

Plan *USA Today* once ran a number of articles about Tiger Woods. One concerned Tiger Woods when he was a young man—how he put up a plaque on the wall in his room that listed all the achievements of Jack Nicklaus.

Anybody who follows golf knows that Jack Nicklaus has the nickname "The Golden Bear." For twenty-five years, he had been absolutely the number-one name in golf. He's got more major championships than anyone else—eighteen, I think. He's the best of the best.

Tiger Woods' plaque showed all of Jack Nicklaus's accomplishments: how many amateur titles he had won, how old he was when he won his first major, how old he was when he won his career grand slam, how many majors, and tournaments, and dollars in earnings he had. All this stuff.

The fact is that Tiger knew what he wanted to do from a very young age—he had a plan. In order to be sales champions, we also have to know what we want. We have to do what Steven Covey says: "Begin with the end in mind."

Have a plan. Know where you're going. It's called a "strategic sales plan."

Let's look at these words one at a time. "Strategic" means that we are taking into consideration the big picture factors that might affect our business. "Strategic" means that we understand the economic and environmental climate, we understand our competition, we understand our marketing position, we understand our own strengths and weaknesses, and we know what type of business we're likely to get from our current customers and what amount of business we need to create on our own.

"Sales" means that it's a concept that is all about selling. It's not a marketing plan, it's not an operating plan, and it's not a business plan. It's how we're going to maintain and grow our sales.

The final concept is "plan." If you don't know where you're going, you'll probably end up in a place you never intended. So the saying goes. A plan based on sound strategy and focused on sales will get us where we need to go. At over the age of fifty, my ability to again get my marathon time under three hours is going to depend to a large extent on my ability to put together a sound plan. Planning is what helped me attain excellence in running in 1991 and planning is going to help me be excellent in 2005.

Sales practice is the essence of implementation. Sales practice is the execution. Sales practice is getting out of the stands and into the game. Sales practice is doing the activity every day that (when tied to an effective sales process, and based on a sound plan) will guarantee that we will be the best salespeople we possibly can.

What's in your strategic sales plan? You have to understand many things to have a good strategic sales plan, including:

- How much business did you generate from your current clients last year?

- How much business are you expecting this year?
- What type of prospects are you going to go after this year?
- Who are your key accounts?
- Who are your targeted key customers?
- What type of revenue can you expect by geography, by industry, and by type of product and service?
- What are your annual goals?
- How are you going to break it down into quarterly targets?
- What's your monthly plan?
- What do you have to do every day in order to implement this plan to ensure your success?

If you're Lance Armstrong, do you wake up one day and say, "Oh, I think I'd like to ride in the Tour de France. What's that date in July? I'll just show up at the starting line on July 3, 2004."

Well, obviously it's not like that at all! You have to, he has to, we all have to prepare. Where do you want to go? How are you going to get there?

I'll tell you right now I'm looking to get back to the form I had in 1991, when I looked like and ran like an elite marathon runner. I was 38 then and weighed 127 pounds. My body fat was under 10 percent. I was up to between seventy and ninety miles a week. I had everything planned out by the month, by the day, by the week, and by the year.

In 1991, I had eleven consecutive races where I set a PR (personal record). This was at distances from as little as 5K, where I went under 17 minutes at the age of 38, to the marathon where I ran a 2:53. I was 208th out of 6,500 runners at the age of 38.

As I reflect on why I was good, it came down to preparation, and now I'm starting to get back to that same type of mindset. We'll see where it takes me. We'll see if, with good planning, I can get back to that same level of fitness fifteen years later.

Practice Practice, practice, practice. You certainly can have an identifiable, repeatable, measurable sales process. You can sit around all day long and prepare your sales plan, but like everything in sports, business, or life, you've got to get out there and practice it.

Larry Bird, the great Boston Celtics basketball player, was once in a slump. He's one of the greatest shooters ever to play the game, but he hadn't been shooting well in his last four or five games. There are people who play the game for ten years and become half as good as Larry Bird, but he hadn't been shooting well and, for him, that's a slump.

So what did Larry Bird do? He went back to the fundamentals. He went to the arena and he shot ball after ball, hour after hour.

What about Lance Armstrong, from the cycling analogy? People ask, "Lance, how come you're so good at what you do?" There's a commercial that Lance is in—I think it's for one of the shoe manufacturers or a sports drink—in which he looks right in the camera and says, "My butt's on my bike six hours a day." That's his edge. He trains; he practices.

Marathon runners put in 70, 80, 90, 100-mile weeks. What about selling? What's the practice? What's the practical application of selling?

It's taking action, making the calls—spending the time, as it were, in the saddle. It means keeping track, keeping score, following up, making sure you're doing the things that you know are going to make you successful.

Isaac Stern, the great violinist was once asked, "How do you get to Carnegie Hall?" Do you know what his answer was? "Practice, practice, practice." Here he was in his nineties and he still practiced up to six hours a day. When someone said, "You're a maestro. You're a virtuoso. People come from all over the world to hear you play. Why in the world do you have to practice?" With a twinkle in his eye, he said, "You know, I think I'm getting better." Practice is what it's all about.

ASK THE SALES DOCTOR

QUESTION

Terry writes from Birmingham, Alabama: I've been a teacher for many years and I am entering a career as a salesperson in my late forties. Am I too old to be a successful salesperson?

ANSWER

I think teachers make great salespeople. Much of what is involved in being a professional salesperson is educating and then inspiring or motivating people to make choices. And what better background training, in order to be successful, than being a teacher? Teachers educate their students and inspire or motivate them to be successful in any different array of subject matters. Also, teachers have to work with a wide variety of people from diverse backgrounds. Teachers have to be excellent at listening and observing body language, eye contact, and all the types of soft intuitive skills that sales people most envy about teachers. I think teachers make great salespeople.

Overcoming Obstacles

Why Salespeople Fail

It breaks my heart when I hear about salespeople leaving their jobs. Most of the time, the person hasn't left because he or she was a bad salesperson or that it was a bad company to work for. Nor do they leave because their competitors are stealing too much of the business and the market opportunities just aren't there anymore. The three major reasons salespeople fail are all tied to issues that we've been carrying around since childhood:

1. Salespeople fail because they have some type of crisis that affects their belief in themselves.
2. Salespeople fail because they won't prospect.
3. Salespeople fail because they won't ask for the order or the commitment.

"It is hard to fail, but it is worse to never have tried to succeed."—*Theodore Roosevelt*

A Belief System Crisis The first reason for failure is all about not having the right attitude. I'm talking about self-esteem, enthusiasm, persistence, optimism, consistency, empathy—a person's feelings and beliefs. When I first interview a salesperson who is not doing well—whether it's a salesperson at the top of his game who suddenly runs into trouble, or someone who is struggling to get started—I always begin by asking questions. I want to find out if something happened that has affected their emotional strength.

"To be a champ you have to believe in yourself when nobody else will."
—*Sugar Ray Robinson*

Let me give you an example. About ten years ago, I was working with a large investment banking firm in a large Midwestern city when one of the firm's salespeople approached me. At first glance, the man appeared to have it made. He was a top producer in his industry, having been the number one salesperson for eight of the last ten years. He could donate a lot of money to his church, which was very important to him, and at the same time pay for his children's college tuition. All of his dreams had come true.

But then he put several of his best clients into a stock that tanked. The value of the stock dropped from $60 a share to zero in a weeks time. The loss was an enormous blow to this man, and his beliefs failed: he no longer believed that he was the best investment banker for his clients, nor that his company had the best products and services. And because of that crisis in his confidence, he was afraid to get on the phone and explain to his clients what was happening. Before long, most of his business—or "the book" as it's called in the investment banking business—started to dissipate in front of his eyes. I had been quite surprised when the man asked to meet me off-site at a restaurant about twenty miles from his office—that's how embarrassed he had become regarding what had happened to him.

We talked for a long time during that first meeting. I asked him to think back to what had made him successful in the past and what was going on in his business now that might offer him a glimmer of hope that there was something left that he could do. We continued to meet for breakfast over the next several days, and slowly he was able to rebuild his confidence and then he was able to rebuild his business. He brought in a younger junior broker who had a lot of enthusiasm, and together they rebuilt the book within a year. Three years later, he was right back on top, the lead salesperson in the company.

You can see that this man's selling skills weren't the problem. He failed temporarily because he had a crisis of belief. It can happen to anyone, and it happens often enough that it is a common reason why salespeople are no longer successful. Make sure to keep your beliefs strong and in focus during the length of your sales career.

No Prospects Failing due to a lack of prospects is directly related to selling skills. If it becomes chronic, it can result in absolute failure in your selling career.

> "The only place you'll find success before work is in the dictionary."
> —*May B. Smith*

When you don't have enough prospects to call on, you become paralyzed by objections and rejection. Perhaps you can't overcome a current customer's resistance to expanding their order. Or maybe something comes up with a prospect, an objection that you can't answer or you can't face. In either situation, you walk away weaker in your ability to be successful with your next customers and prospects. Your activity levels go way down, and you're at the mercy of customers who want you to cut your prices or enhance your service for free. Selling becomes joyless. And let me tell you, if you're not having fun in your sales career, consider that a big red flag. You're doing something wrong and you're about to go out of business—you just don't know it yet.

Let me tell you about another salesperson I worked with, one in a Southern city. This gentleman too was a top-rated salesperson in his company. His problem grew out of the fact that 50 percent of his business came from one client, and over the years he had developed a very high level of distaste for the buyer of this particular account. They didn't see eye-to-eye on anything—the weather, politics, food, business practices, whatever. They were polar opposites.

His bigger problem, though, was that it had been so long since he had done any prospecting that he felt totally dependent on this particular account. One day he called to tell me he was going to leave his company and find work in a totally different industry. I was shocked. When I asked him why, he said he no longer wanted to work with the client who was giving him such a hard time. He didn't know how to go about building the business to replace that one client. He was actually going to leave an entire industry because of one customer!

I took him to the library and began to show him how to go about identifying prospects in his territory. Working with the business librarian, we were able to collect various directories that listed the best prospects for him based on the discussions he and I had about his business. To further identify groups of prospects, we also looked at trade publications, daily newspapers, and specific publications focused on his industry. We talked about the best type of prospects for him and whom he'd been successful with in the past. You could just see the excitement start to build. As he looked at his territory, he identified companies he hadn't been to in years, as well as many he had never contacted at all.

Eventually the man recognized his real problem: he didn't have enough prospects, but he could easily solve that by scheduling the time to go out there and start calling on some of these new or inactive clients. It became clear then that he no longer had to depend on this one unpleasant account. He could build his business to the point that he could take the risk of trying to change that relationship or just simply walk away from it. And, indeed, that was what happened. He had a falling out with the buyer, but because he gained several new accounts, he was able to walk away from the business.

The story doesn't end there. When the owner of the account company found out why the salesperson and his buyer had parted ways, he fired his buyer and brought the salesperson back in. Talk about a sweet ending. Not only did the salesman rebuild his business by making sure he had sufficient prospects, he was able to win back the large chunk he had been willing to walk away from.

Not Asking For a Commitment The third reason salespeople fail is probably the hardest to diagnose, but it has the most power to enhance our business once we recognize it. Most salespeople fail at getting business because they are not willing to ask for it! They are perfectly comfortable, way too comfortable, presenting their company's products and services. They just keep talking and talking and talking and talking, and they don't give the prospect a chance to make a decision. The only way to find out if you are close to getting the sale, the appointment, or finding out if the prospect understands your offer, is to stop talking and ask a question.

I have to admit that this was my problem when I was first starting out. Luckily, shortly into my career, I had a very experienced sales manager work with me. After accompanying me on a couple of calls and seeing my results over a period of several months, he told me, "Warren, you're not a professional salesperson. You're a professional visitor."

Professional visitors talk, talk, and talk, then they go back to the office feeling great—"Oh, I'm going to get this. I'm going to get that." But they never bring the business in the door because they haven't stopped to ask for the commitment or the order.

> **"Courage is the moment when an ordinary being becomes an extraordinary being."—Brian Jacques**

Some of you who are new to sales might be thinking that you could never be that direct and ask these hard questions—that it would be manipulative or pushy. But asking for a commitment or an order has nothing to do with being manipulative. It has nothing to do with pressuring people. The reason we ask commitment questions is to give the buyer or the prospect an opportunity to stop and think about it. They really have to say to themselves, "Do I want to buy this product? Do I want to work with this person? Is this the company I'd like to partner with?"

Unlearn Before We Can Learn

I've given these failure factors a lot of thought over the years. Why do we sometimes have a crisis in belief? Why won't we prospect?

Why are we afraid to ask for the order or the commitment?

The answer came to me on an airplane when I was traveling between speeches. I was reading a science fiction novel. In the book, the scientists had created a wormhole and they were able to go back into and compress space and time. They were also able to go back in time and watch themselves and other people.

That's what clicked. I starting thinking what it would be like if we could go back into the past. Maybe we could discover why we find it difficult to ask people to do things. Why we are not willing to prospect. Why these crises in belief happen sometimes. The more I thought about it, the more I realized that what we fear is that very small word that begins with "n" and ends with "o." We're afraid of "no."

I decided that this fear of no is the number one enemy of sales-people. I think it goes back to childhood when we were conditioned to believe that "no" is bad.

Think about it. Imagine you're a two- or three-year-old toddler again. Toddlers like to explore. Everything is fascinating, from the dirt on the floor to the cat's litter box. Imagine you're in the kitchen of your house and your family is making dinner. Tonight is spaghetti night, but of course, you don't know that. You just hear all the sounds and see things going on in your toddler way, and you walk toward the stove. If your family has electric power, you see a red glow; if it's gas, you see a blue flame. Both are fascinating in their own right. But in addition to the fascinating blue or red light, you also see this large metal pot that's kind of shaking on the stove. You don't know that it is water boiling in the pot. What grabs your attention is the sound of the boiling bubbles coming from this shaking metal object on top of this really cool blue flame or red glow. You want to see what that is, so you reach up for that pot.

What would have been the scenario in your house? Would your mother have had an intellectual discussion with you about the properties of water and the propensity of very hot water or steam to inflict great damage on the epidermis? I don't think so. She yelled "No!" at the top of her lungs.

Imagine how many experiences like that taught you to associate the word "no" with your bad behavior, even before you were aware of what rejection is really all about. We are so afraid of the word as adults because we've been conditioned from a very young age to associate whatever results in a no to be bad.

> **"A winner never quits, a quitter never wins."**
> —*Unknown*

Now fast forward to your life as a salesperson. We are asked all the time to go out there and face no. Would you like to get together this week? No. Have I earned the right to your business? No. Who else besides you gets involved? No one, or I'm not going to tell you. Will you buy this product from me? No.

Even if you're good in sales, you're going to hear "no" about half the time. But it's *not* bad! *You have to unlearn this.*

Here's another thing we learned as a child that we need to unlearn as an adult. How many times did your parents tell you, "Don't talk to strangers?" Think about this. From a very young age, your parents, your teachers, your aunts, and uncles all told you not to talk to strangers. Now as an adult salesperson focused on building and maintaining your business, you're asked to go talk to as many strangers as you possibly can. Is it any wonder that we don't want to prospect?

> **"The world is your playground. Why aren't you playing?"**
> —*Ellie Katz*

We all have negative thoughts embedded in our consciousness. And sometimes we need to unlearn them to become a better salesperson—not learn, but unlearn. Think about that. Think about what you can unlearn to become a better salesperson. Think about how our entire profession can learn by unlearning.

Unlearning Myths

The Myth of the "Natural Born" Salesperson In addition to the three major reasons why salespeople fail, there are a few others I need to discuss. The first is falling for a common myth.

I once was a parent chaperone for some young children who were waiting while their older siblings took part in a gymnastics meet. We were in a room adjacent to the gym so that the younger children would be out of the way of the event. There were about thirty children and a handful of adults. One child, Johnny, was the most energetic, outgoing, talkative child imaginable. Whether speaking with other children or an adult, he was a gifted conversationalist. One of the other adults turned to me and commented that Johnny was a "natural-born salesman; he'll be great in sales because he is such a good talker." This adult didn't know me and didn't know that I was a sales trainer and speaker. I had to chuckle to myself. Once again, I had run into an intelligent adult who believed the myth that as long as you are a good talker, you will be a good salesperson.

Being an excellent salesperson is not about the gift of gab, nor do you have to be born to it. While it's true that every rule is proven by the exception, in almost all cases that I know about, it was an understanding and application of the universal, underlying principles of sales that guaranteed success. If you don't have the skills and knowledge, you won't succeed as a sales professional.

The Myth of "Sales Cannot Be Reduced to a Process" Another one of the myths about selling goes like this: "Selling? Who needs a process?"

> "Be a good listener. Your ears will never get you in trouble."—*Frank Tyger*

I'll just wing it.

I'll just go with the flow.

I'll just shoot from the hip.
I'll just create it on the spot.
I'll just go by the seat of my pants.
I'll just say whatever comes into my mind.

How many times have you heard that type of language when you hear salespeople describe what they do? Well, it's wrong. Great salespeople don't shoot from the hip, wing it, or say whatever comes into their mind.

Great salespeople are light on their feet and flexible. That's a great attribute to have. Generally speaking, though, the greatest salespeople have a sales process that they follow.

When I say "sales process," I'm talking about something that is definable, actionable, measurable, and repeatable.

Once, when I was speaking in Jacksonville, Florida, a man in the back of the room raised his hand when I described how I was trained (the "Go-get-'em" model, which means no training at all). He said, "I have a sales process. It's really simple, Warren. It goes like this: find a need. That's my first step. I go out there and I find people who have needs. And my second step is to fill those needs."

Everybody in the audience kind of laughed, but I thought it was a great statement. I found out later that this guy was the top salesperson in his company. He has a definable, measurable, repeatable process: "Find a need. Fulfill the need." It's pretty simple.

The Myth of "Selling as Telling" "Selling as telling" is another myth that can result in failure for the salespeople who believe it.

There are many paradoxes in sales. One is that because the companies we work for have great products, which they do, and wonderful services, which they do, and tremendous guarantees and warranties, which they have, our job is to show and tell. Demonstrate the product. Present the solution. Tell our customers what they need.

This paradox is the 80/20 rule, known as the "Pareto Principle." In 1906, Vilfredo Pareto (1848–1923), an Italian economist, observed that just 20 percent of Italians owned 80 percent of their country's accumulated wealth. Pareto's Principle states that a small number of causes is responsible for a large percentage of the effect—at a ratio of about 20:80.

What this means for salespeople is that 20 percent of your talking will result in 80 percent of people telling you what they need—and that when they talk 80 percent of the time, you only have to talk 20 percent of the time.

We can see from these above examples that there are reasons why salespeople fail. We can call these the salesperson's sickness. Do you know what the cure is? It's understanding the principles of Total Selling. Once we master the three

> **"Shallow men believe in luck. Strong men believe in cause and effect."**
> **—*Ralph Waldo Emerson***

Ps, we will have the antibodies to overcome the illness. We will have the answers that explain how to overcome the failures that we face and turn lemons into lemonade.

Later in this book, you'll learn more about how to ask the right questions. Here I want to focus on how the myth of selling as telling can lead to failure when salespeople reverse the 80/20 rule.

When I go out in the field and work with salespeople, I'm always amazed that they think that they are spending from 30 to 50 percent of their time lis-

> **"Success is 99 percent failure..."**
> **—*Soichiro Honda***

tening to their customers and prospects. But I've surreptitiously timed many of these meetings, and believe me, it is closer to 20 percent.

A few years ago, I was in the field with a young man in an affluent city in Florida. Before we went in to see a tremendously important potential client, we sat in the car and rehearsed the great questions he was going to ask. The prospect was the best prospect for this salesperson in the entire state of Florida. Imagine my horror then when the young man talked steadily the first fifteen minutes of the meeting! Obviously uncomfortable, the buyer looked at his watch, shifted his position in his chair to face away from us, and crossed not only his arms, but his legs as well. Needless to say, the buyer was getting restless and defensive.

I was going crazy. I didn't know what to do. Should I interrupt him? Should I stand up and jump up and down? Finally, I kicked the salesperson under the table. It worked. He looked at me in shock but at least he stopped talking.

I immediately took control of the meeting and started asking the potential buyer questions about himself, his company, his situation, and the like. Over the next forty-five minutes he told us everything we needed to do to earn the right to his business.

When the salesperson and I got back to the car after the meeting, I asked him how he thought the meeting went. "Oh, it was great!" he told me. "Did you see how much information *we* got?"

I replied, "Yes, I saw how much information *we* got. What do you think the first part of the interview was like?"

"Common sense is not so common."—*Voltaire*

"Oh," he said, "it was great. Did you see all the rapport we built up with him?"

I was just amazed. Even though I kicked him, he still didn't realize that he spent the first fifteen minutes of that important meeting talking about himself, his company, his products, his services, his clients, and his applications. Unbelievable.

Selling is not telling. Selling is asking. The salesperson who doesn't understand that might as well look for other employment.

ASK THE SALES DOCTOR

QUESTION

Stuart called from Portland, Maine, asking: Why is there such a negative connotation in the business world when people think of the profession of selling?

"Decide where you want to go in life, then draw a map to get there."—Success Tip

ANSWER

Many people in sales exhibit behaviors that are self-centered, arrogant, and obnoxious, and that is why there are negative stereotypes about salespeople. This has been reinforced by the media over decades and generations. The true sales professional is one who is there when the customer needs them, is able to make promises that are delivered upon in a timely manner, tells the truth, and develops long-term relationships. This is contrary to the stereotypical fast-talking, make it happen at any cost, transactional type salesperson. This is not what professional salespeople do, so do not be concerned about that negative stereotype.

Unlearning Negative Stereotypes

Every time I open a program, whether it's a business speech, a forty-five minute inspirational speech, or a one- or two-and-a-half-day program, I always begin by saying, "Let me ask you a question." This is after I've been introduced: "Warren's a sales expert. He's been doing this full time since 1987. He's an excellent salesperson. He was a fantastic sales manager. He's been in the business for twenty-seven years. He's a bestselling author. He's the host of a weekly radio show *Total Selling with Warren Wechsler* that's heard all over the country." After I am introduced, I stand up in front of this crowd of anywhere from fifty to fifteen hundred people and say, "Thank you so much for that kind introduction. Let me ask you a question. Has anybody in the room ever had a negative experience with a salesperson? Can you please raise your hand?" You can imagine how many hands go up. Then I say, "Has anyone ever had more than one negative experience? Can you raise your other hand?" And we get two arms up. I then say, "Has anybody ever had three, four negative experiences? Can you get your legs up in the air? Can you levitate for me? Get all your appendages up there!"

After the laughter dies down, I look at them and I say, "You know, it's interesting. In the sales business we have this tremendous opportunity to educate and inspire people about how wonderful our business is. We can help buyers buy. We can help people solve problems."

"To give anything less than your best is to sacrifice a gift."—*Steve Prefontaine*

When you and I think about the sales profession, when average person on the sidewalk thinks about the word "salesman" or "saleswoman," all these negative stereotypes come back. We think about the time the salesperson lied to us. We think about the time the salesperson was unprepared. We talk about the time when the salesperson overpromised and underdelivered. All these are standard myths about all salespeople that haunt the sales profession. Is it any wonder that we as sales professionals struggle with the honorable nature of our profession? We too have had those experiences. Even though we are well-educated sales professionals, we tell the truth, and we make reasonable promises and overdeliver, we are still haunted by these images. Total Salespeople, by their actions, defy these images and raise the professional bar for all salespeople.

Why Total Selling Works for all Salespeople

Before concluding Chapter 1, let's look at three different classifications of salespeople and why *Total Selling* will work for each type.

Underperformer

You may be what I call an underperformer. If a reasonable standard for someone in your business is $1,000,000 worth of business per year, we have established the minimum acceptable level of performance.

What if you are a salesperson who is annualizing at the rate of $600,000 a year? You are an underperformer. And in that case, you need the most day-to-day counsel; you need to learn and be accountable for daily selling activities; you need to take the most active role in your career success.

Managing your activity is the key. "Activity" means:

> **"The man who rolls up his sleeves seldom loses his shirt."—Thomas Cowan**

- How many new contacts did you attempt in this reporting period?
- In the last week, how many new people did you contact?
- How many decision-makers did you actually get a hold of?
- How many new appointments did you have during the previous week?
- How many product presentations did you make?
- How many needs analyses did you do?
- How many times did you ask for the order?
- How many times did you get the order?
- How much business did you write?
- How many referrals did you ask for?
- How many referrals did you receive?

These are all measurable statistics that you need to track to achieve success.

Underachiever

The second category is called the underachiever. Let's say you've got a million-dollar territory and you are bringing in $1,000,000 worth of sales. But you know that with the right amount of self-motivation, adjustment, or self-management, you might actually be a 1.3 or 1.4-million-dollar salesperson masquerading as a one-million-dollar salesperson. Now look at the productivity you get if you could figure out a way to achieve more than you are achieving today.

A reason why people fall into this underachiever category is that they've reached their comfort zone, and based on the way they're being paid—either through commission, salary plus commission, incentive, bonus, or whatever—they're doing just fine and they're not really inspired to do any more. If that's the case, you have to figure out a way to strive for new goals to accomplish in your life and then tie your performance to achieving more each day.

The underachiever needs less statistics-oriented assistance, so you can work on high-level skills such as sales planning skills or key account management. You can work on and open some of these large accounts that nobody else seems to be able to.

Overachiever

The third category is called the overachiever. This is the person who's already doing 1.3 or 1.4 million dollars in a $1,000,000 territory. You're consistently a top performer.

Many times the top performer seeks the newest ideas to stay ahead. Overachievers are looking for ways to remove roadblocks. Overachievers like being recognized as having the most advanced skills regarding how to do more in less time, how to leverage relationships for referrals, and how to work major accounts more effectively.

Total Selling will guide you, counsel you, and inspire you to think bigger and set larger targets—no matter what type of salesperson you are. Most people respond to challenges. They want to know they're doing a good job and they want to be happy doing what they're doing. My role is to constantly challenge you to understand what type of salesperson you are today, create a blueprint for self-improvement, and act on it.

> **"I've got a theory that if you give 100 percent all the time, somehow things will work out in the end."**
> —*Larry Bird*

Why Constantly Improving Your Skills is Important

Even though I have been in sales for over twenty-five years, on any given day, you might find me reading a book about professional selling, listening to an audio tape program about sales, or attending a sales seminar. Why do I do this even though I am an expert in the profession?

If we have muscles that we don't exercise, they stop working. When we stop doing sit-ups and crunches, our stomachs get soft. When an equipment manufacturer invents a new machine to improve our abdominal muscles and we either don't know about it because of ignorance, or we choose to ignore the new technology out of stubbornness, we lose either way. Our sales muscles are exactly the same. We must be on the lookout for new ways to conduct our business and adapt the new ideas to our sales careers.

I am always looking for ways to improve my skills. I have a saying: "If we're not getting better, we're actually getting worse." If we're not constantly figuring out ways to move ahead in our business lives, we're actually falling behind; we just don't know it yet. If I can pick up one new idea at a public seminar, by

> **"The man who does not read good books has no advantage over the man who can't read them."**
> —*Mark Twain*

reading a new book, or by listening to an audio program, I feel that I have invested my time wisely.

This is the end of Chapter 1. We have just begun to explore the concepts of Total Selling. As we begin this journey together, I hope to share ideas that will inspire you to the highest level of achievement you could possibly imagine. Who knows, you might even exceed your own expectations once you embark on the path to being a total salesperson. Let's begin.

Part One
Sales Process

Chapter Two

Building a Strong Foundation

You've Got to Have a Sales Process

"The only good comparison is comparing yourself against your own potential."—*Success Tip*

People have probably been thinking about the topic of the sales process as long as people have been selling. Every salesperson must have a process. Yet, many people think that they don't need to have a system in place.

You might say, "Oh, sales is not linear. Sales is seat of the pants. Sales is go with the flow. Sales is do what comes naturally." This is a bunch of nonsense.

Imagine if you were the builder of an office building and your approach was to tell your architect and construction manager, "Just go with what you feel. Just wing it. Go from the seat of the pants. Do what comes naturally." You wouldn't want to even stand in the lobby of that building, would you?

Sales is the same way. You have to have a strong and reliable process to ensure that your sales structure won't collapse. Let's look at the sales process and its important elements. First, the sales process needs to be *measurable*. It's very important for salespeople to have an understanding of where they are within their own process.

- Are you doing the proper types of activities?
- Are you doing a sufficient quantity of activities to ensure the success of your sales plan?
- Are there milestones to show you if you need to be working harder, smarter, or doing more of one thing, less of another, or about the same with another action?

Another aspect of having an effective sales process is that the sales process is *repeatable*. If we do something one way one time and another way the next time, it is like recreating the wheel each time. Why not establish how you will go about building and maintaining your business? We need a model with distinct steps that are repeatable; that can be implemented, monitored, and tracked.

Finally, my ideas on the sales process differ from others in that everything that I stand for is based on *activity-based selling*. In other words, if it isn't a "do this," "call him," or "write her," then it's not an activity. And if it's not activity-based, it's not really a sales process.

Process as a Pyramid

Envision a sales process with the structure of a pyramid. Our sales process needs to have a strong foundation to ensure success.

Activities that involve building a prospecting list and sorting through it to make sure the people and companies we are talking to are valid prospects are examples of activities that form the base of the pyramid. People and companies either exclude us, or are excluded by us, and so fewer people take the next step up the pyramid. This is repeated as we move through the sales process, until only a few of the people and companies we started with at the base of our pyramid are still with us when we get to the top.

Inbound Versus Outbound Sales Processes

Here are two examples of what I mean when I say "sales process." In the *inbound model*, whether its customer service sales, inbound 800 sales, or retail sales, for example, some of the activities might

> **"A winner never quits, a quitter never wins."**
> **—*Unknown***

be: greet the customer, ask questions to establish needs, present the solution based on the needs, and then ask for the commitment.

What we have just described is a four-step process that meets all of the criteria we talked about earlier. The process is measurable. You can know:

1. How many people you greet on a daily basis;
2. How many people with whom you conduct a needs analysis through questions;
3. How many people you present to based on the needs analysis; and,
4. How many people you ask to buy.

The four steps I've just defined can be done over and over and over again—they are repeatable and they are activity-based. It's not a psychological model nor is it an emotional model. It is absolutely activity-based.

The inbound model of selling is unique in a number of different ways. Number one, it is reactive, meaning that in most of those environments you are awaiting the customer or prospect to call you. This is the case in inbound telesales, in retail sales, and in customer service-type sales.

Another unique aspect of inbound selling is that you are interrupted, which is contrasted to the outbound model where you, the salesperson, are interrupting other people. A third distinction of the inbound model is that most of the people qualify themselves—

instead of you having to get an appointment with them, they are getting an appointment with you by showing up or calling you.

SALES IDEA

Turning the inbound service-oriented call into a selling and referral opportunity

The inbound service call is a great opportunity for us. It gives us a platform to showcase our value and be of service to our customers. It gives us a chance to discover additional selling opportunities. Here's how to do it.

Always take care of the customer's needs, issues, and concerns that caused them to call in the first place. If the customer is calling because of a problem and we can solve it, doing so creates goodwill that can lead to open mindedness on the part of the customer.

If the outcome of the inbound call is positive, then ask if they have a few more minutes to talk. It's OK to ask for permission. After all, this is a customer and we want to be sensitive to any time constraints.

Let's look at the *outbound model* for a different example of a sales process. Some of the activities involved in a reasonable outside sales process are as follows:

- creating a list of prospects or clients
- contacting those prospects and customers to ask some basic qualifying questions
- understanding how we set appointments
- understanding the prospects' needs through asking good questions and listening to the answers
- presenting our solution based on their needs

> • asking for a commitment
>
>   As you can see from this model, it's very similar to the inbound model except for two very important distinctions: 1. the outbound process is proactive, and 2. the outbound process is interruptive.

Whether you are involved in inbound or outbound sales, the main point to understand is that whatever your sales business is, it's paramount to have a sales process. Once we grasp the concept that the best way to think about business is through a sales process, we can move on to the next step of deciding what our sales process will look like.

ASK THE SALES DOCTOR

QUESTION

Here's a question from Bob in Chicago: "I'm an inbound salesperson who is moving into an outside sales position. I'm concerned that the skills I've developed as an inside salesperson won't translate into success as an outside salesperson. Is this correct?"

The greatest thing in the world is not so much where we stand, as in which direction we are moving."—Holmes

ANSWER

No. The only difference between the inbound and the outbound model is the way that initial discussion starts with the customer or prospect. On the inbound side you are available to your customers and prospects and they engage you. In the outbound sales world there is more rejection because you as the salesperson have to go out there and start the discussion, start the introduction, or arrange the appointment. After that, the skills of listening, providing great solutions and asking people to make decisions are same. If you are dedicated to your profession, you believe in your company's products, and you can work with the fact that you're going to face more rejection, you can make the transition easily from inside to outside sales.

Actually, inside sales people have to be much more disciplined about the way they manage information because they are constantly being bombarded and interrupted by a wide variety of shifting priorities and needs. The outside sale person often times has much more control over that. So those skills you've developed as an inside salesperson are actually putting you at the head of the class when you transfer into outside sales.

The Evolution of a Customer

The first stage in developing a customer base is to start with the biggest picture possible, the "universe of prospects." What this means is that we put together the largest list of potential customers that we could possibly come up with, utilizing criteria that are important to us. For example, we might utilize criteria including geographic territory; the size of company; the type of decision-maker we would like to contact; and a particular industry group with a certain number of employees. Then we develop our master list, our universe of prospects.

Now it's up to us to qualify the prospects, to sort out the wheat from the chaff. Not everyone we put on the list even offers us an opportunity as a prospect. In fact, we may decide, during the sifting process, that we never wanted to work with many of these people in the first place. This is not a "sour grapes" response to the situation. Do you remember Aesop's fable of the fox and the grapes? The fox kept leaping up toward the tree to try to get the grapes, but was unable to reach them. So he finally decided that he really didn't want those grapes anyway because "they were sour." No, if we discard a prospect at this stage, we have a legitimate reason to do so (and that's good).

The Funnel and the Pipeline

To visualize the evolution of a customer, I'd like you to imagine a funnel. In this funnel, the "universe of prospects" we just discussed is at the top. The next level down is stage two: "interested prospects." These prospects are people with whom we've had contact and who seem to have some interest. The main condition for a prospect to be in this category is that we've actually made initial contact, either by phone or in person, and there seems to be a reason for both parties to move forward. Stage three involves clients with whom we are qualified to establish a successful relationship: qualified prospects.

ASK THE SALES DOCTOR

QUESTION

Fred from Flint, Michigan writes: "I've been working with a particular buyer for many years and I know there is another person in the organization that has the authority to move more business to a company like mine. Every time I ask the person I'm working with, I get the response like, 'Well, Joe is not really involved and everything goes through me.' I know this company buys close to a million dollars of my product every year and I'm getting about $50,000 of that business. What can I do to get more business?"

ANSWER

You are in a position of having high risk and potentially having high reward. If you have been "blocked" by a lower level decision-maker, you have two options; you can either say to that person "Look, I think I've got more value to provide you; how about if I bring my boss to meet with you and your boss?" You raise the level of commitment on both companies' parts so that your particular decision-maker doesn't lose face. The risk is that the person feels you're being too pushy and you end up getting less business. In the case you have described you have very little to lose. A riskier strategy is just to call that hidden decision-maker directly and let them know that you think you have value to provide and also explain that you think that you've been "blocked" by this person and you're wondering what you can do to unblock that path. This is a very risky proposition, but you will have very little to lose if you are getting hardly any of the business.

When you imagine this funnel, it is broad at the top and narrows down to the smallest point on the funnel—a tube. So prospects enter the funnel from the top, the "universe" level, and start to narrow down to "interested prospects" in the middle. As we learn more about these interested customers and their needs, and we begin to feel that our solutions match up quite well, they become more and more "qualified" and move further down the funnel into the tube. This component of the funnel is actually what I call the "pipeline." In the pipeline are those very qualified prospects who have a keen interest in working with us. We can divide the pipeline into three segments.

The first segment is the "cool prospect." Cool prospects usually feel low urgency or feel that it's not very important to make a change. They seem to have an interest, yet they may have a good relationship with their current vendor, be in no hurry to make any changes, or be happy enough with their current situation. Yet they're open to new ideas, and they might be convinced to change something in their situation that would enable us to earn all or part of the business.

The second segment of the pipeline, moving down, is the "warm prospect." There was an urgent *or* an important reason for them to make a change that includes us. This prospect obviously is more exciting, and in these cases we're looking at an opportunity, depending on the sales cycle within our particular business, that would come our way within a short time frame.

For example, let's say your sales cycle tends to be six months to a year in building from beginning to end. A cool prospect would be in that one year time frame. A warm prospect would probably be between three to six months of making a change.

Now we move down to the bottom segment of the pipeline—these are our "hot prospects." These are people who are looking to make a change, because there is some reason for change that is urgent *and* important. There is something going on that is giving us a great opportunity to get this business.

The "hot" part of the pipeline is where most salespeople spend most of their time, because the hot prospect is about to become a customer. Generally speaking, if we use that sales analogy of having a one-year sales cycle, these are people who are going to be making their decision to move business our way in the next thirty, sixty, or ninety days at a maximum.

SALES IDEA

MONEY IN MOTION

Whenever a company that you've been calling on changes their purchasing decision-maker, there's an opportunity that I call "money in motion." You might have a situation in which you have not been the dominant supplier because the person who makes the decisions is a very loyal customer of one of your competitors. When this changes, we have an opportunity to get to know the new person and sometimes an unlevel playing field becomes level.

Now, the downside to "money in motion" is this: if you're the incumbent who has a very strong relationship with the purchasing decision-maker, the new employee sometimes makes changes just for the sake of change. So, money in motion is a double-edged sword. It's exciting when we're the "new kid" and a change is made in our favor. It's less exciting (and it can be terrifying) if we are the incumbent and a change is made, especially if we never saw it coming.

Action: Find an account, either a current customer or a prospect, where a person has retired, been reassigned, or let go and put "money in motion" to work.

Wave Theory

Because prospecting is such an integral part of being successful in a sales career, we often think in terms of direct correlations between our outbound proactive efforts and the results that accrue to us. Often, this is not the case. Yet, it's important not to be disillusioned about the effects of prospecting but to understand what is really going on.

"You are never a loser until you quit trying."
—*Mike Ditka*

For example, once we understand how much new business we need and how much contact we need to make in order to hit our sales goals, we need to allocate the time to make those calls. In my business, for example, I set aside one-hour blocks of time and schedule as many of those blocks during a week as I need—depending on how much business is already coming in the door and how much business I need to find.

This is where the theory of waves comes into being. Bear with me here; it's kind of an out-of-the-box thought.

If you are looking at a still lake, you would say there is nothing happening on the surface. Now, imagine if you tossed a pebble into the center of the lake. Some waves will be created. Will a wave make it back all the way to shore? No.

Now, take all kinds of pebbles, rocks, and large stones and throw those into the lake. You could generate a little bit of wave patterns and maybe one of those waves will break toward you on the shore. Tossing rocks and pebbles into the lake is analogous to our outbound efforts.

Here is where the wave theory comes into play. Sometimes the wave hits on a different shore first. In other words, we might be calling into the manufacturing industry in the Midwest in order to build our business, and then seemingly out of the blue we get a call from the distributor market in the Southeast. In this case, we might say, "Gee whiz, outbound prospecting doesn't mean a thing because the business came from a totally different source."

Here is the secret: If you never made the outbound calls to manufacturers in the Midwest you never would have received that call from the distributor in the Southeast. I can't explain it. I've practiced it at least a hundred times over a fifteen-year period and I know that when you send out the energy—when you throw the rocks, stones, and pebbles in the lake that you're looking for business in—the wave will break back at you. You just never know if it going to hit from the left, the right, or from straight in front of you. That is wave theory.

SALES IDEA

TEAM UP
Synergy is a concept that teaches us that one plus one does not have to equal two. It could equal three or seven or even eleven. Synergy means that the sum of the parts can often be more than we might expect.

For professional sales people in an organization that has more than one area of expertise, this can be a huge benefit.

Why? People buy from people who they like and trust. And at least 85 percent of our current clients already like us, trust us, and are open to new ways that we can be of service.

A great way for a company to grow revenue is to add additional lines of business to a current account. This is so obvious, yet many times it is over looked. There are numerous examples of add-on or cross selling opportunities.

Action: Contact an associate in your organization and share information and ideas on how you can synergistically grow each other's business.

Your Customer is Your Best Prospect

Customers are the lifeblood of everybody's business. They pay our salaries; they help us succeed. When they buy from us over and over again, they validate everything that we work for. Let's talk briefly about broadly classifying what kind of current or future opportunity your relationship with your customer actually is.

There are three basic types of relationships that we might have with our current customers. Categorizing these relationships helps us know how to focus our energy and time.

"Go-To" Opportunities

In the first scenario, we are the go-to supplier for our customer base. We're capturing 80 percent or more of the business and, obviously, we spend a lot of time with this type of account. The next type of relationship is a customer who buys some of their products or services from us, typically less than 50 percent. We are not the go-to source. In these cases, we spend a lot of time talking to the customer; trying to figure out where we are in the relationship today, how we need to position ourselves to improve our position, and how we're going to move our business from where it is today to where we'd like it to be tomorrow.

SALES IDEA

USE "NOW," "WHEN," AND "BY THE WAY"

If they say yes, say, "Great, there are three things that I'd like to discuss. What can I be doing for you *now*?" (Look for current opportunities—additional business.) The open-minded nature of this question often helps the client discover ideas we never would have thought of ourselves.

If no *now* opportunities appears, move on to "*When* might I be of service to you again?" (Look for future opportunities, threshold events in their business, new programs needed, and new people to meet.)

If no *when* opportunities surface, it's still OK. If there are *when* opportunities, make the appropriate follow-up action. Then move on to, "*By the way*, here is a new idea that you might consider and we can discuss an add-on or cross-selling idea," or move into a referral request: "*By the way*, who else in their company we might speak to about additional products or services that we can provide?"

Action: The next time your best customer calls, implement this approach.

The third type of customer is the one with whom we've never been the go-to supplier, or in which we were the go-to supplier in the past. This is an account in which we're getting zero to 10 percent of the business. If this is a large account that has enormous potential, then this is a terrific place for salespeople to spend a lot of their time. There is a tremendous amount of opportunity and leverage to grow an account that buys 5 percent or 10 percent of what they could buy, to one who is buying 20 percent, 30 percent or even 50 percent from us.

The definition of a "go-to supplier" is simple. When your account is ready to buy, are you the first or second person they "go to"? If you are the first, then you are a go-to player. To put this in perspective, if you already are the go-to supplier for a particular customer, then your opportunities within that account are maintaining the business you have and growing the business through expanding your products and services—or, better yet, through referrals you might receive simply by asking your customer. If you are in a relationship with the second type of customer (the customer from whom we are getting less than 50 percent of their business) our opportunity is to position ourselves to be the go-to source. We might grow our business through developing new relationships within the account, by competing head-to-head against entrenched incumbents, or by finding brand-new ways to add products and services to that account. Finally, in the third type of relationship (where we have never been or in which we were once the go-to supplier), once we figure out that there actually is an opportunity there, it is well worth our energy to develop that account. We can have lots of growth where there previously was zero sales volume. You can see that understanding how to rate yourself with your current customers can give you a tremendous advantage in terms of where you ought to focus your sales process activities.

Give Your Best to Your Best

A sound sales process begins with an understanding of who your best prospects are. Your best prospects are not perfect strangers. They're not prospects whom you have identified as targets. Your best prospects are your current customers.

A current customer is nine times more likely to buy something from you than the person who has never bought from you before. They have crossed the most important threshold that any prospect ever crosses when they decide to do business with you or your company. That is, they like you and they trust you.

The fact is that you could basically reach every goal you've ever set for yourself by taking care of your current customers. This presumes you have current customers. If you're starting a brand new territory or if you're starting something from scratch, you are going to be forced to go out there and talk to perfect strangers all day long. That's not the case for most salespeople, however. Most of the time, either we inherit a book of business that's been built that we have to grow, or we are the entrepreneur or the salesperson in a territory and we've grown that book of business ourselves.

The main reason to keep in touch with your current clients and focus on them as your best prospects is that you want to do your best to retain their business. The converse of the fact that it's nine times easier to persuade a current customer to buy from you, is that it's nine times more difficult to persuade someone who has not done business with you before to do business with you now. A *retention strategy*, therefore, is the number one reason why you want to keep in touch with your current clients.

In fact, in most businesses, 75 to 80 percent of their sales come from the repeat purchases of current customers. Let's look at a hypothetical salesperson that does $2,000,000 in sales in the year. In the following year, probably up to $1,600,000 of that $2,000,000 would come from repeat business from current customers.

ASK THE SALES DOCTOR

QUESTION

Tammy, an industrial saleswoman from Florida, asks, "Is
it OK to call my current customers over and over again to
offer them new ideas and products?
Sometimes I feel like I'm wearing out my welcome and
should focus on new accounts instead."

> "If there's a job to be done,
> I always ask the busiest man in
> my parish to take it on and it
> gets done."—Beecher

ANSWER

The answer is yes. Obviously, you should be calling on new
accounts. There's no doubt that a key to being successful in
sales in the long run is making sure you have a really strong
and consistent flow of new customers for your business. So
it goes without saying that you ought to focus on new
accounts. However, it's not new accounts *instead*, it's new
accounts *in addition* to my current accounts. So yes, you're
right. You ought to be thinking about new accounts.

Let's go back to the main focus of your question. You call
on your current customers. You call them over and over
again. You're introducing new ideas. And you're wondering if
you are wearing out your welcome. Well, let me tell you
something. It's OK to go back to your current customers and
offer them new products and services. I have done a lot of
research on this. Many buyers say, "My vendor doesn't call
me as much anymore. My supplier seems not to be as interested in my business anymore." You have to be calling your
current customers. They want to know what's new. They want
to know what's up. They want to hear from you.

Are you wearing out your welcome? I have to answer
with a question. Have they told you that you're wearing out

your welcome? Are they saying, "Call me next week. You really don't have to call me every week." Or, "You don't have to call me every month. Try every other month." You are wearing out your welcome. When you offer these new products and services on a regular basis, are they buying them from you? If the answer is that they are, then obviously you're not wearing out your welcome.

Maybe this is what's really behind your question. Are you facing the law of diminishing returns, where you're calling your customers over and over again and you're finding out they're buying less and less, or picking up fewer and fewer new ideas? If that's the case, then maybe your intuition is telling you you're wearing out your welcome and you need to focus on new business to grow your business. As long as they're listening to you and they're accepting your ideas, and sometimes they buy and sometimes they don't, then I think you've got the appropriate approach to calling your current customers.

Say you had a route-selling type business selling potato chips, and every week you came back to replenish the stock of potato chips. And then pretty soon you introduced taco chips, and after that you introduced corn chips. That would be the same type of thing: "Here I am again. Do you want to have some corn chips? Do you want some potato chips? Do you want some barbecue chips?" It would be offering the new products and services to your same clients over and over again for years.

Too many times, in the sales business, we ignore these customers in pursuit of the brand-new prospect. In fact, somebody once told me a story about one of their top customers. This customer stopped doing business with them because they felt that they weren't being serviced by the sales professional that was calling on them.

That sales professional may have missed appointments, not

delivered on promises, or maybe he was just focused on new business and not taking care of the current customer.

What we do know is that the customer decided to cut way back on what they were buying from this particular company—not because the product was bad, not because the application of the product was bad, but only because the salesperson stopped calling on them. Retention is the number one reason to take care of your customers.

To leverage this philosophy with your best clients, take the top 10 percent of your client base and call them your high A's, your top customers, or your Circle of Excellence—whatever you'd like. Make a determined effort to keep in touch with those people on a regular basis, whether it's once a month, once a week, or once a quarter. Do something special for the top 10 percent of your customer base. Invite them to events, ask them out to breakfast, go to their facility and take a tour, invite them to your facility and give a tour, take them to a Rotary meeting, take them to a ballgame, or bring them some bagels. Do whatever you can to nurture the top 10 percent of your clients because it will pay off in spades.

Avoid the Candy Factory

I'm reminded of the *I Love Lucy* episode where Lucy and Ethel are trying to make money. Remember? This is the 1950's when Ricky and Fred, who are Lucy and Ethel's husbands, were the guys who made the money and Lucy and Ethel had to stay home. They were always looking for ways to scheme and make money. There was one episode where they went to work in a candy factory. Initially they were wrapping candy as it came down the conveyor belt. They were able to wrap it and put it in the box, wrap it and put it in the box. Pretty soon, the conveyor belt started moving faster, and they couldn't wrap them fast enough. They started eating them, chewing them, stuffing the candies into their dress, down their pockets, wherever. It was hilarious how fast the candy factory conveyor belt started moving. It was ridiculous. Pretty soon the candy was flying off the end.

Now I've been told that as a salesperson and a sales educator, I have a warped sense of humor. And I do. When I think about that episode of *I Love Lucy*, I think about the sales profession. Too many times we spend our energy going out to get that new business, and we completely ignore our current customers. When a competitor of ours calls one of our current customers and says, "I've got an idea for you," our client is thinking, Why hasn't my current vendor, the incumbent, the company I've been loyal to told me that or asked me that? Why do I feel left out, ignored, or under-utilized? That's what they're thinking. They are the older candy falling off the conveyor belt.

Your best prospect, folks, is your current customer.

Don't Talk Yourself Out of Another Great Prospect—The Lost Account

"Have a belief in yourself that is bigger than anyone's disbelief."—*August Wilson*

I was traveling with a salesperson in North Dakota who sold construction tools. He did new tool sales, rental, repair—all the things you see on a construction site: hand tools, power tools, scaffolding, ladders, safety equipment. As we were driving around this individual's territory I kept seeing these huge jobs with a trailer parked nearby and a general contractor's name on it. The first time I saw that trailer I said, "Is that one of our accounts?" He said, "Well, no, I haven't called on them." I thought maybe they're a small contractor. We arrived at a school, and there's the same general contractor's name. Five minutes later we were in front of a big addition to a large manufacturing plant, and sure enough the same general contractor's name had been painted on the trailer.

"OK," I said, "how large is this contractor?" It turns out it was the largest contractor in his territory and he had never called on them.

I asked, "Why is that?"

"Well, I heard we used to do business with them about fifteen years ago, and they were unhappy with us and stopped buying from us."

"Fifteen years is a long time. We should probably go back."

You could just see the fear in his eyes. Why would we go back and call on a customer that had a bad experience with us fifteen years ago?

The point here is that man sold tools. Who buys more tools than anybody? General contractors, mechanical contractors, electrical contractors—anybody on a job site buys a lot of tools. Strategically it had to be a good fit, and in this case it was a tremendous fit.

I asked, "What do you know about this company? What would you say when we went in the door? How are you going to introduce yourself? What are you going to say about your company? What are you going to take with you? Who are you going to ask for? What resistance are you likely to hear when you get there? How are you going to handle it?"

He reported, "I'm going to tell them who we are, what we do, the fact that we work with many people like them in similar businesses. I understand that we did business with them a long time ago, and if there was a problem I'm here to make sure I can take care of that. Or if there are new people around who have never heard of us, I want to start over again and develop a relationship. I want to start from scratch."

"When we go in there," I said, "we want to find out who is the controller; who is the CFO; who is the VP of operations; and who is the general manager. Those are the types of people we're looking for." Aim high, and you will be amazed at how much information you can get once you reach the original person you're looking for.

We introduced ourselves to the receptionist who was very kind. She had even heard of our company. We asked for the general manager. She walked around the corner. Our salesman was fidgeting. He wasn't sure what was going to happen. A man walked out and said, "Oh, I've heard of your company. I wondered whatever happened to you folks. It seemed like you fell off the face of the earth a long time ago. You always had a good reputation around here. I wonder why you stopped calling on us."

Can you imagine? Here was a salesperson that had driven by that company based on hearsay and innuendo that they had a bad experience over a decade ago, and he had been afraid to make that call. This man said, "Bring me your current catalog. Give me all the information. I know there's a need. We've got a bunch of new jobs coming up. We worked with you successfully in the past. We should probably get started again."

Lost accounts are a great opportunity for salespeople to build or rebuild their business. In many cases, the lost account is more of a negative issue in the mind of the salesperson than it is in the mind of the lost account. I've had many instances in which salespeople told me they had an account that used to buy but doesn't anymore—there was a big problem, things got real ugly, and therefore they hate us and they're not going to buy from us anymore.

In many of these cases, I say, "Let's go see them!" Why? Because the opposite of love is indifference, not hate. If they loved you before and they hate you now, at least there is some emotion there.

The best thing to do is to apologize. Let the customer work through his or her feelings to reach an understanding. At that point you're at least back to neutral and you can start to rebuild the relationship. Don't neglect lost accounts.

Qualifying Our Prospects

Once we decide that we will approach a particular prospect or customer for additional business, or that we will attempt to revive a lost account, it's important to recognize that there are four specific attributes that qualify prospects as *valid*.

These four attributes actually can represent different people within an organization. In many small companies, all four attributes will be vested in the same person; in larger organizations, we might find that one or two people possess parts of one or two of the attributes. We might need to become acquainted with five, six, or eight people within a company to know that we have all the people involved who can make decisions on behalf of the company. Let's look at these four attributes one at a time.

"A genius is a talented person who does his homework."—*Thomas Edison*

The first attribute of a qualified decision-maker is determining if the person has the "need" for our product or service. This is the person who actually uses our products or services on a day-to-day basis. Most important, this individual needs to find solutions that will help him or her do the job more quickly, easily, and/or safely, and make sure the company is not falling behind competitors.

The second attribute of a qualified decision-maker is his or her level of authority. This is the person who has the ability to make a decision for companies to actually move forward. This person is often the owner of the company or the highest-level decision-maker at a particular division or operations area of a company. This person makes the important decisions that will move the company forward strategically.

This person is often interested mainly in "the big picture." He or she views the business from high above and is not as interested in the day-to-day tactics. This type of decision-maker will often ask such questions as, "Will this decision make the company faster, better, or more profitable?"

The third attribute of a qualified decision-maker is whether or not that person controls the money. This is the person who actually pays the bills. Typically these individuals are purchasing managers, purchasing agents, or accounts payable managers. This person is most interested in getting the best value for the company's money. This does not mean that he or she is always looking for cheap solutions and the lowest price. Often, this person knows that you get what you pay for, and he or she is just making sure that the company is spending its money wisely and receiving the maximum value for every dollar invested.

The fourth attribute of a qualified decision-maker regards an individual we might not think about immediately. This person is called our "champion." This is a person who may not actually have the authority to get things done within a company, yet is so committed to our solution that they he or she is willing to carry our flag into the company to make things happen. This person is often a decision-influencer as compared to a decision-maker.

SALES IDEA

FINDING ALLIES

One of the easiest ways to lose a sales opportunity is to mistreat the people lower on the organization chart. Most people look past the assistants, receptionists, and decision-influencers to force access to the decision-maker. This is inappropriate.

Treat all assistants, receptionists, and decision-influencers as important people who have a real role to play. Always find out their names and then call them by name every time you see them or call them. Appeal to their sense of fairness and their desire to help their company.

Action: Show respect to the next three: assistants, receptionists, or decision-influencers, and watch your influence soar.

A decision-influencer is someone who has the ability to get the right people's attention, to work out problems as they arise, to generally be our guide within a company. What's important to a champion is to make the company look good and to make sure that he or she maintains personal status. This type of person is generally risk averse, yet in some cases they are extreme risk-takers and are known for it. So we need to figure out the type of champion with whom we are working as we approach a company.

"He that is overcautious will accomplish little."
—J.C.F. von Schiller

The title of this chapter is "Building a Strong Foundation." Having read it, it's easy to see that these ideas—relating to your prospect base and the type of business you're in, understanding the funnel concept, understanding how to qualify your prospects and customers—will lead you in the proper direction in your sales process. This strong foundation is going to be the structure on which we build the following steps. These initial ideas are somewhat akin to doing your homework or doing detective work. In the next chapter, you learn how to approach customers in the right way while continuing to build on this foundation.

SALES IDEA

CALL YOUR BEST PROSPECT NEXT
Many sales people save their best calls for tomorrow. Yet, tomorrow never comes.

Many sales people find that when they finally get around to making the best call, they are "a day late and a dollar short."

The best way to overcome this habit is to make the next call the best call. What do I mean? I mean to act as though you can only make one call and then your time is up. Your phone goes dead. You're out of quarters.

Write down the name of your very best prospect. It could be a current account that you want to sell additional service to, an inactive account that you want to reestablish a relationship with, or a brand new prospect that you are calling for the first time.

Commit to approaching your best prospect before you do anything else. (And before your fiercest competitor does it before you!)

Action: Make the call now. Don't hesitate. Pick up the phone.

Chapter Three

The Rest of the Story

Paul Harvey is arguably the most famous radio news reporter of all time. He has another story-oriented program he created called "The Rest of the Story." In it, he lays a strong foundation, helps the listener get comfortable with the direction of the story, and then, after a pause for a word from his sponsors, he completes the program by telling the rest of the story.

Getting Out There

In the realm of the sales process, what we're about to talk about now is the rest of the story. As we mentioned earlier, building a strong foundation is the best way to begin our sales process. At this point, having identified who our best prospects are and how companies make decisions, it's time to actually pick up the phone, knock on the door, or get in the car and make the attempt to get a face-to-face or phone-to-phone conversation with our prospects and customers. Selling begins when a buyer and a seller are interacting. Let's get started.

ASK THE SALES DOCTOR

USING LETTERS OF INTRODUCTION

Dan writes, "What is the best sequence to use when approaching a new prospect? Should I mail or email a letter of intro-duction, send information on my company, call first and then mail a letter? It's all so confusing.

> *"A good plan executed right now is far better than a perfect plan executed next week."*
> *—George S. Patton*

ANSWER

I'm going to answer your question in a number of different ways. The first thing is to make sure that you're targeting the right person. You said in your question, "Should I call first and then mail a letter? Should I send a letter? Should I mail or email information?" The first decision you have to make is who in the world are you targeting at that company?

My research has shown that up to 50 percent of initial calls are actually made on the wrong person, somebody who either doesn't make the decision, can't make the deci-sion, won't make the decision, or doesn't have a need. So what I usually do is I call companies and I say, "Here's who I am, here's the company I represent. The reason I'm calling is I'm trying to find the person why buys blank, purchases X, whatever." And I also say, "This would be the person, if your company was going to make a change, would be involved at the highest level. If your company was changing strategy, this person would be involved in this type of decision."

Now the reason I say it that way, Dan, is that I want to make sure that I'm aiming high enough in the organization that even if the person turns out to be too high, they're going to refer me to the person in the organization who is at the appropriate level. So make sure you're targeting the right person, but don't be afraid to aim a little bit high.

As far as "should I mail a letter of introduction or shouldn't I?" I've been asked this question I can't tell you how many times at the seminars I conduct all over the country. The answer is so simple. You have a list of prospects. Let's say there are fifty names on the list. I hope you've got more, but let's say you've got fifty. Maybe you have 500. Take fifty names that are similar in everything. Similar in size, similar in geography, similar in the level of decision making you're aiming for. Take your best letter of introduction, a business card, and mail or email information to half the names on that list. And then, the other half, don't do anything. Wait 48 hours, longer if you're sending them out of your direct marketing area. In other words, if you're in Philadelphia and you sent all of them to Philadelphia, wait 48 hours. If you're in Philadelphia and you sent them all over the country, wait 72 hours because it's going to take another day for the mail to get there.

On the day, that is, either 48 hours or 72 hours from the time you sent the information, pick up the phone and at the same time call one from column A and one from column B. At the end of all fifty of those approaches, look at the results. And ask yourself; was it better for me to send information and then call? Or did 99 percent of the people not even see what I sent them? If you do it this way, Dan, you'll know exactly what you need to do. And you'll know if you should spend your company's money and send out information.

You also said, "Should I send out information on my company?" Let's remember one key fact, people buy from people. So don't use your company's marketing materials and flyers and corporate brochures and line cards indiscriminately, because most of the time they get tossed in the trash. Most people don't read what you send.

> If you can capture people's email addresses on the front
> end of those conversations, send an email that doesn't look
> like junk mail. The recipient will open it up and look at it.
> And amazingly enough, they'll respond and either tell you
> they're interested or send you to the right person.

The Preapproach

Once we establish how decisions are made within a particular company, the next step is to figure out how to tactically approach this
opportunity. It's important to understand that the Boy Scouts
motto ("Be Prepared") applies to this situation. Research the company, its market position, its current vendors, and its market
environment. Do not overlook this step.

In this day and age, with so much information technology at our
fingertips, it is incumbent on us to know as much about the company as we can. This is not to say that we hesitate to make the
approach because we're waiting for more information before we
proceed. We just must be sure to do our homework, and walk in
with an understanding of what the company does, who their customers are, who is likely to be our competition, and what the
company's potential needs might be.

Initial Approach

As the sales process moves forward, now that we know who the
players are and something about the company, it's time to make
our initial approach. In many cases, this means making a phone
call to one of the people we've identified as a decision maker
within the organization. In some cases, even though doing so
seems to have become a lost art, the initial approach can actually
be a face-to-face visit to the company without an appointment.
The best way to begin a face-to-face initial approach is to prepare

yourself emotionally and mentally to greet a stranger for the first time, making that stranger feel comfortable and warm about your entering their premises. This means you walk in with an upright posture, a smile on your face, and a confident attitude.

"Faith that the thing can be done is essential to any great achievement."—*Thomas N. Carruther*

Next, immediately look to see who the receptionist or administrative assistant is and approach that person, observing the events going on in front of your eyes. If the telephones are ringing off the hook and people are making many demands on the receptionist, you wait quietly until there is a lull in the action. If it seems relatively quiet you simply walk up, introduce yourself in a very clear and direct manner by telling them your name, and the company you represent, and ask to see the person who would be involved in strategic decisions that are related to the product or service that you are offering. If you are then told that the person you want to meet with only works by appointment, you simply hand the receptionist your card, and ask for the card, telephone number, or email address of the person you would like to see. Then tell the receptionist/administrative assistant that you will be calling this person for an appointment in the future. Thank them for their time and don't forget to get the name of the receptionist or administrative assistant. When you make a telephone call to that company at a later date, you will be the one in one thousand salesperson who, when the receptionist answers the telephone, is able to greet that person by name.

In any event, we have to remember that every time we make a contact with a customer or prospect, we have to have a very clear objective in mind. I call this idea "ECHO", which stands for "Every Contact Has an Objective". We have to be willing and able to fill in the blank in the following statement: "The reason I'm calling you today is..."

Too many salespeople beat around the bush or try to sell their products or services during the initial approach. We should instead focus on getting the face-to-face appointment (in outside sales) or on getting the appropriate amount of time with the customer or prospect (in outbound telephone sales).

We have to make sure that whatever statement we make about why we're approaching the prospect for an appointment takes into consideration what is important to them and offers them clear benefits. Imagine if I called you up and said, "I want to meet with you because I want you to make some money for me." Would that be an appropriate way to approach you? Of course not.

Yet so many salespeople lead with "Me, me, me" and "My company this, my company that," instead of leading in terms of what's important to the customer. Examples of initial benefits that customers or prospects might respond to include:

- increasing profits
- improving their process and/or productivity
- saving time
- getting a competitive edge
- lowering overall costs of doing business

These are ways to get the attention of the people that we're talking to as we speak in terms of what's important to them.

The Appointment: Setting the Stage

After the reception area, what do you do next? Make sure you fully introduce yourself to the person you are meeting. You're going to be a stranger in their environment. Let them know who you are and whom you represent. Give them a glimpse of what you do. Provide a five or eight or ten word opening so they know what your company and what you, particularly, are all about.

In a face-to-face situation, ask, "And what's your name? Oh,

Dolores? Hi, Dolores. It's really nice to meet you." Ask and repeat their name.

SALES IDEA

ENLISTING AID

A great strategy with receptionists who are hesitant to help you on the initial approach is to ask them to do you a favor. Say, "I'm trying to contact somebody I've not talked to before. Can you help me out?" And don't forget to say thank you. It's the most important thing that you can do on the initial call.

Action: On your next approach, ask for a favor and say thank you.

How about an icebreaker statement? Especially in the face-to-face call, don't do something really predictable, like see a fish on the wall and say, "Oh, wow. People in your company really like fishing, don't they?" That kind of comment is contrite and overused. If there's been a heat wave in your area, say, "Gee whiz, is it as hot today as it was yesterday?" Or if you've just had some rain say, "Wow, did you get a lot of rain where you live? We sure got a lot where I live." The weather is a really interesting and fun thing to talk about. If there's a really popular sports team in town, you can use that as an icebreaker. Just do something to warm up, to develop some type of common ground.

ASK THE SALES DOCTOR

THE "NO SOLICITING" SIGN

Paul writes, "I want a new terri-tory and my manager won't give me one. All of my prospects have 'No Soliciting' signs posted and only see people by appointment. After I make my calls on my current accounts, I have no way to make initial contacts. How can I grow my business if I can't make new calls?"

> *"Obstacle: something you see when you take your eyes off your goal."*
> —*Wise Word*

ANSWER

I actually called Paul and talked to him. I felt empathy for him after I had a chance to talk to him, so I want to make sure that his question gets answered. I'm sure many of you face the same thing.

First, you have to wake up and smell the coffee here. When people put up "No Soliciting" signs in their business, they're not trying to keep out professional people. I know from talking to you, Paul, that you're selling a business-to-business product with a service that's highly sought after, very much needed, and a very important part of what business people are looking for.

The reason people have those signs on the door is they want to keep the people out who are selling the velvet Elvis posters. "Oh, there was a fire in the warehouse, and we've got velvet Elvis posters to get rid of cheap." They're trying to keep out the people that come in with this little bottle and spray it on your carpet and say, "Yes, it's the magic cleaner." And what you don't know is the bottle they're using is a hundred times more concentrated than the one you're going to buy.

These are the types of people signs are trying to keep

out—door-to-door salespeople, peddlers, people who are not really legitimate.

Conversely, you, Paul, are a sales professional. And the reason you're in those buildings is to introduce yourself to people in the building while you are calling on your established customers. Since you were in the neighborhood, you just happened to stop in to introduce yourself to potential clients in the same geographic area.

That's what you're doing. You're not soliciting. Soliciting is when somebody calls you at home during dinner and tries to make you switch long distance providers.

One of the most exciting times in a salesperson's career is when they are in front of a new prospect for the first time. Yet this is where many salespeople make huge mistakes and lose great opportunities to be successful. Why? Because, too many salespeople do too much of the talking too much of the time. There is a tendency to talk about ourselves, our company, our products, our benefits, our services, or our solutions before we've taken the time to find out more about the customer and his or her needs, concerns, and issues.

"My greatest strength as a consultant is to be ignorant and ask a few questions."—*Peter Drucker*

This sounds completely ludicrous, yet I have observed this type of behavior again and again in the field: salespeople spend way too much time talking about themselves and way too little time talking about the prospect and his or her needs.

I have found a cure to this disease. It's called "The Two Minute Drill."

The Two-Minute Drill At the initial appointment, every single buyer or prospect is asking themselves three questions about you, the person sitting in front of them. They are asking 1.) Who are you? 2.) Why are you here? and 3.) What's in it for me? What they are looking for is to find out if you are the person that has three very important attributes that they seek. They want to know if you are competent, if you have integrity, and what your intentions are.

That's why every time when I meet with a new prospect I make the following statement: "You're probably wondering just who we are, why I'm here, and why this is of any interest to you at all, right?" I have noticed people over the years actually nodding their heads while I make this statement, and even when they're not giving me that body language cue, they are certainly nodding their heads emotionally because that's exactly what's on their minds. They want to know who the heck are you, why you are there, and why they should care about it in the first place.

"Sincerity and truth are the basis of every virtue."
—*Confucius*

The Two-Minute Drill is literally two minutes or less. So, after you make the comment "You're probably wondering…," you then move on and say, "Let me share with you for two minutes what my company does, who I am within the company, what we do for our customers, and what we might be able to do for you; then I want to spend the rest of the time talking about you, your needs, your concerns, your current situation, your likes, your dislikes, your unmet needs; and if there is something that we feel is important for us to continue talking about after that, if we agree that I have something to offer you, then by all means let's see if we can continue the discussion. How does that sound?"

When you approach people this way you will be amazed at how many times you get more information that you ever could imagine.

ASK THE SALES DOCTOR

QUESTION

Phil from Seattle asks: "Warren, I spend a lot of time working on large accounts and I'm wondering if major account selling is any different than traditional selling?"

ANSWER

Phil, this is a great question. In some ways it's quite different. There are many decisions that need to be made in order to pursue large account opportunities successfully. Large accounts present a number of different challenges. For example, they typically involve multiple decision-makers, the sales cycles can be rather lengthy, and there is an intense amount of competition and a lot of downward pressure on pricing.

When you're going after major accounts, it pays to think and act as an underdog. Don't presume that because you have a strong relationship, or because you're the incumbent, or because you have a perceived competitive advantage, that you are in the driver's seat. In fact, many things happen that could change the direction of major account pursuit and it is always important to think as if you are losing. This is not to say that we feel paranoid or under confident. What it does mean is that we have to act *as if* we are always in an underdog position. This keeps us hungry, alert, and able to make decisions quickly.

Take Control of the Meeting

"People who say it cannot be done should not interrupt those who are doing it."—*Unknown*

You will find that you have built up a great rapport with people after you lead the appointment with your Two-Minute Drill. It's important now to remember that even though the meeting may or may not be at your location—it might be at the office or a restaurant—it's still important for you to think and act as though you are the host. Your job is to make people feel comfortable; be the master of ceremonies, so to speak, and make sure that you are keeping track of the time, bringing people back to the appropriate subjects when needed, and generally moving the meeting along in the appropriate manner. Much of this will happen naturally once you learn to ask the right questions. Making people feel comfortable and asking the right questions are the keys to controlling the meeting.

SALES IDEA

SETTING THE STAGE FOR GREAT INITIAL MEETINGS

"Begin; to have begun is half the work. Let the half remain; again begin this and though wilt have done it all."—Ausonius

There are three questions every prospect/buyer needs answered before they are open to a dialogue with a sales professional. They are:

- Are you competent?
- Are you credible? (Do you have integrity?)
- What is your intention in meeting with me?
  Too many times, we are in such a rush to tell our story

and sell our services that we get ahead of ourselves and miss the opportunity. Symptoms of this malady include:

- Lack of rapport at initial meeting
- Prospects/buyers who don't open up to you
- Meetings that end prematurely
- Lack of appropriate information sharing

We want to open the meeting appropriately to make it memorable and unique. Until we answer the three questions that are in the front of the prospect / buyer's awareness, we're just like all the other people who call on them.

Action: Open your meeting with the following: "Thank you for the opportunity to visit with you today. You're probably wondering who we are, why we're here today, and why it may be important to both of us to have a dialogue."

"Let me spend two minutes sharing some background on my company and my background, some companies like yours that we have helped, and some of the reasons that companies work with us. After that, I'd like to spend the balance of our time together exploring what your situation is and what potential next steps we might take. OK?"

Asking the Right Questions

In the 1970s, there was a TV show called *Colombo*, starring Peter Falk as a bumbling, rumpled-jacketed detective. While Colombo's manner was disorganized, he solved the murder every week. His key to success was his famous ability to ask the right questions. He never presumed that he knew anything.

He was like a good doctor: he asked questions and listened. He used the "Socratic Method." So why don't we do that? Why don't we ask more questions? It's because we think we have to have all the answers and so we lead with our presentation before we ask the right questions. This is like putting the cart before the horse and it is a tremendous failure on our part.

What are the right questions? There are basically four areas that we should talk about when we are in a meeting with a potential customer.

"The word LISTEN contains the same letters as the word SILENT."—*Unknown*

What Do You Have *Now*? The first series of questions all revolve around the *current situation*. These are questions such as:

Who are your current vendors?

What type of products does your company buy?

What type of services is important to your company?

How often do you buy?

What exactly do you buy?

How long have you been buying this product or service?

What is your relationship with the current vendor and your salesperson?

How long have you been in this position?

What's important to your company?

What are you trying to accomplish?

What are your goals?

You get the gist. Be curious and interested in what the situation is within the company. It's presumptuous of us to think that we have the right solutions before we even ask the questions. To do that would be like going to a doctor and having them look you up and down as you walk in the door and say, "Yup, knee problem; get over here, we're going to replace that knee right away!" when you came in because your neck was out of alignment. It's absurd, a doctor would never do that, and we shouldn't do it either.

What Do They Like *Best*? The second series of questions should revolve around *what they like best about their current situation.* You might say, "Warren, that's ridiculous, they're going to praise their current vendor and we'll affirm why they should keep buying from them!" Well, you're right and you're wrong.

You're right because, yes, they should be telling us the things they like about the current vendor and you're wrong because it's not going to hurt us. It's going to allow us to see where our products and our offerings match up based on the things they like about what they're doing right now. It also shows that we're not there to try to slam a solution down the prospect's throat, but that we're really interested in what they find successful in their current situation.

ASK THE SALES DOCTOR

QUESTION
From Toronto, Betty writes: "Is it really appropriate to ask the customer what they like about their incumbent supplier? It would seem to me that just encourages them to talk about a situation that works well for them, and talk themselves out of being open to new ideas."

ANSWER
You might think that once they start talking about their current supplier and how much they provide and what the value is that that is actually closing the door to you. In reality the person develops more respect for you because you are willing to listen to what your competitor provided to your customer or prospect. You also ought to be taking mental or

written notes so when it is your time to talk and present your solution, you can refer back to the points they made about the things that satisfies them or the benefits they enjoy in working with the incumbent supplier. The best reason to ask the "What do they like?" question is that it opens the door to ask the "What do they like least?" question which is the most penetrating question of all. Once people are comfortable that they've had a chance to tell the good things about their current supplier, they are much more willing to describe the chinks in your competitor's armor. This is the main reason why we lead with "What do you like?" and then segue into "What do you like least, or what do you dislike?"

What Do They Like *Least*?

The next area we need to probe is *dislikes or unmet needs*. This is really where the rubber starts to meet the road when you're interviewing your customer to see if you can be of service. We really need to know what some of the areas are upon which we might improve.

Now there is a very interesting way to approach this subject. Instead of saying, "What do you hate about your current vendor?" or, "Where are you not having your needs met?" we have to be more subtle and less confrontational. The best way to ask this question is, "Tell me what you like least about your current situation.", or, "Can you give me some idea where the service your current supplier provides to you could actually improve?"

Now when we ask these two questions we're actually getting to the issues of dislikes and unmet needs, yet we're asking them in a more profound and less threatening way. We make it easy for the customer to respond.

What Would They Want in a *New...*? Now we get to the forth and most important part of our *needs analysis* of the customer or prospect. In this step, we want to know what is going to cause him or her to make a change. So we need to find out what he or she would want in a new relationship, a new vendor, a new product, a new service, or a new solution. The operative question is what would he or she want that is *new?* We're looking to discover why the prospect or customer would make a change now and why he or she might want to make a change in our direction.

One of the best ways to ask these questions is to say, "Now you've been working with the ABC Company for how long, and you've been in business for how long?" Then you ask, "When you made the change to ABC Company in the past, why did you do that?" What we're trying to find out is why he or she made the change previously. It will give us an indication of why they might make a change in the future.

Or we ask the question, "If you are to make any changes, what would precipitate them, what would have to happen, why would you make a change? What would you look for in a new vendor, a new relationship, a new product, a new service or a new solution?"

Once we understand how to ask questions and listen to the answers, we are going to be so much better than our competitors who call on them. Prospects will remark to us on how amazingly positive the interview was and how they have never been approached quite like that before. When this happens, you're really in the realm of professional selling.

ASK THE SALES DOCTOR

THE NOSY SALESPERSON

Jeannette asks: As a financial advisor I have to ask people some pretty nosy questions. This is easy to do after I've developed some level of rapport and trust, but that takes time. Sometimes I find myself taking the time to develop a high level of rapport and trust with someone who then doesn't even have money to open an account with me. How do I keep from wasting my time with people who are not real prospects without putting people off by getting too nosy at the beginning?

ANSWER

As salespeople we have to be willing to ask very simple, qualifying questions up-front with people before we get into the rapport building and the presentation. There are very simple things we need to do. There's something about people's money. It's so emotional that we're afraid to ask them to talk about it.

I was working in a large Midwestern city when I was asked to visit a struggling branch of an investment banking/stock brokerage firm and work with the salespeople and find out what they were doing wrong.

I worked with one of their lead young prospecting-type salespeople. This guy knew more about investing than any ten people. He was so friendly and so easy to talk to. I spent about an hour listening to him on the phone. He had boxes and boxes of cards (this was before people computerized their prospecting system). I looked, and he was so persistent and consistent. He talked to the Jones family fifteen times, and the Baker family twenty-two times, and the Whatever family thirty-seven times.

He was very excited about one particular family. I said, "What do you know about these people?"

"They're farmers in Iowa."

"What else do you know?"

"I don't know."

I then asked him a whole host of questions (Do they own their farm? Do they lease their farm? What do they grow? How many acres do they farm? How many children do they have? What type of equipment do they have? How much money do they have?) and to all of them, he responded "I don't know." I then said, "You know what? Give me the card. Let me call Mrs. Jones. I'll say I'm your assistant. Let me ask some questions." He replied, "Go right ahead."

"Hi, Mrs. Jones. I'm calling on behalf of Fred."

"Oh, Fred, that nice young man. I've been talking to him a lot over the last year."

I said, "Yeah, that's one of the reasons we're calling today. Let me ask you a question, Mrs. Jones. Do you do much investing?"

She said, "No." I could tell by the way she answered there was something more behind that.

"Oh, is most of your money in the bank?"

"We don't have any money."

"Oh, really. Why is that?"

She said, "My husband and I have been on disability. We live on what comes from Social Security."

"Let me ask you a question. A lot of the investments that we talk about require people to put up $1,000 or $5,000 or $10,000 or $50,000 at a time if they're buying bond issues. What category would you and your husband fall into."

I was doing this for the benefit of the broker. She burst out laughing. She thought was the funniest thing that she had ever heard because for the last twenty-five years they were fortunate to come up with an extra $5 or $10 at the end of the month. Now, I didn't do that to embarrass Mrs. Jones. I didn't do it to embarrass the stockbroker. But if you are offering a product or a service that requires an investment, wouldn't it be nice to know if people are qualified up front? The answer is yes.

Here's how you do it, Jeannette. All you do is say the following. "Mrs. Jones, our clients basically fall into three categories. There are those fortunate few who can afford to invest..." and then you name a big number. If your top client invests $100,000 at a time, then you say $100,000. "Mrs. Jones, our clients fall into three basic categories. There are those fortunate few that when we bring them an investment idea, they invest about $100,000. Then there's another group of people that invests somewhere between $25,000 and $50,000 with us when we bring them an investment opportunity. And there are those that invest about $5,000 when we present an investment opportunity to them."

So now you've defined, Jeannette, your A, your B, and your C account. And then you say, "Mrs. Jones, which category would you fall into?"

And Mrs. Jones somewhere in central Iowa drops the phone and bursts out laughing, or you might have people say, "Well, yeah, the last bond issue I bought I bought $500,000 worth."

So now they've just told you they're an A. Then you go back to your rapport-building and take the time to develop and all that once you know you have a valid prospect.

That is the easiest and simplest way I can describe it to you. After you develop the initial rapport, you basically say, "Look, before we go any further, I want to talk about a really simple concept..." and you're talking about a business opportunity.

Using Your Eyes, Ears, and ECHO

"Luck is what happens when preparation meets opportunity."—*Elmer Letterman*

It is very important to have an objective every time we make a sales call. As noted earlier, we've called this principal ECHO, which stands for Every Contact Has an Objective. However, sometimes our objective is overridden by the customer's stated or unstated objective. Let me explain.

There are many times when we approach a call with a preconceived notion about an idea, a product or a service that we want to talk about. But, by using our eyes and ears, we notice that we really should be pursuing something else.

For example, I was once working with a salesperson who wanted to talk to a concrete contractor about a particular type of hammer drill. When we went to see the contractor, we noticed numerous tubes of a product called fire stop. Fire stop is a flame-retardant construction product used like caulk to seal around pipes and prevent fire and smoke from spreading. It's a heavily used commodity item on most commercial job sites.

Our objective (to talk about hammer drills) took a big backseat when we saw all these fire stop tubes that did not come from the company with whom I was working. The objective changed to learning the source of the fire stop and asking how we could compete for that business. That's an example of using your eyes and ears and being opportunistic.

Solutions-Based Presentations

Presenting the solution is probably one of the easiest topics to talk about but one of the hardest attributes to put into practice in sales. We in the sales profession spend way too much time presenting. We think we are impressing people so much with our words, products, services, PowerPoint presentations, Web demonstrations, and so on, but this is the area of the sales process that should be kept as simple as possible.

Put in very simple terms, presenting the solution means solving problems. Way too many salespeople use way too many words, talk about way too many features and benefits in the world of selling. The effective route is to find out during the questioning phase is exactly what is on the customer's mind—what their needs, issues, and concerns are, why they would make a change—and then present our solution that matches up with those needs.

If the customer or prospect couldn't care less about how many years you've been in business and how broad your distribution network is, then why talk about this? I've worked with thousands of salespeople in the field and I am constantly amazed at how a simple presentation that should take five or ten minutes turns into a marathon that takes hours. So many times a sale is lost because of over presentation.

Keeping the Presentation Simple Before talking more about solutions, let's say what needs to be said about the use of support materials. Presentation is still critical to winning accounts, but it is a matter of form and substance. Too many companies lead with flashy presentations, leatherbound binders, or exquisite PowerPoint presentations. This is the wrong way to approach any opportunity. The best approach is to walk in with a pad of paper, a pen, and a naturally inquisitive personality.

Be very tactful about visual aids, as well. If you're going to hand someone a visual aid, be quiet while they're looking at it. If someone's making a presentation to you on a new car and that person hands you a sheet of paper, they put you into an immediate conflict situation. You don't know if you're supposed to be looking at the car, reading the paper, looking at the person, or listening to the person.

Some salespeople abuse visual aids. I know there are a lot of marketing people that spend a lot of time and energy making those things up, but remember, they're only tools. My advice is to be careful with the way you use these sales aids. If you want people to listen to you, don't push something in front of them. If you want them to read something, show it to them, then shut up and let them read it.

ASK THE SALES DOCTOR

QUESTION
Dan writes, "I've been told that most people buy for maybe one, two, or a maximum of three reasons. My company asked me to present in a formal manner all the benefits of my company, including the history, the customers we worked with in the past and to me it seems like too much. What do you think?"

ANSWER
I agree with you. I'm a big fan of keeping the presentation simple. Many presentations go too long and are too involved and focus on benefits that are not even important to the customer. I think a customized presentation that responds exactly to the needs that are identified during the questioning phase is the best presentation of all. It's a paradox in sales. You would think that you have to present all your knowledge, or 100 percent of what your company stands for, at every presentation. The truth is that you generally only need about 5–10 percent of the overall knowledge that you bring with you. So keep your presentations short and simple and you will get much more business than the people who are bringing in the leather bound gilded edge presentations that go on into the night.

Presentation Style

"There comes a moment when you have to stop revving up the car and shove it into gear."—*David Mahoney*

We have to be able to deliver a great message that shows the potential customer that we understood their needs. We must deliver a dynamic solution that solves their problems. In addition to the substance of what we're providing, we have to deliver it in a style that is enthusiastic, confident, and filled with images that tell stories (use anecdotes and concrete examples that ensure that the potential customer fully understands what we are offering). In other words, we have to appeal to the buyer both emotionally and logically. One might think that in sales, everything is done coldly, objectively, and based on sophisticated calculations. This is nonsense. People buy from people and the emotional component—giving an appropriate presentation enthusiastically, dynamically, and with confidence—is key.

ASK THE SALES DOCTOR

OPENING A DIALOGUE WITH STRANGERS
Simone writes: What is the best way to open a dialogue with a receptionist who is a total stranger? I spend a lot of time cold calling phone-to-phone and face-to-face. What are your ideas to make these calls easier for me and the person I'm approaching?

ANSWER
Some of the things I'm going to say sound so hokey and so fundamental, you're going to say, "Is that really important?"

And the answer is yes. I wouldn't tell you if it weren't important.

The first thing you have to do when you're approaching a new person whether it's phone to phone or face to face is relax. Let your shoulders relax. Let your face relax. Don't be uptight. Just relax and put a big smile on your face. We have to emotionally prepare ourselves for this conversation we're about to have with a perfect stranger.

The initial goal is to make sure the person will be happier when you're done than when you started. Now don't read into that the wrong thing. They're not going to be happy because you're done (a little salesperson humor there). What it means is that if someone is in a neutral frame of mind when you begin, they're going to be smiling when you are finished because you've created a situation where they're basically happier having had a chance to meet you. The way you do that is by being warm, engaging, and empathetic. Be sensitive to your environment. If there are a lot of phones ringing off the hook and it's a face-to-face call, let that person get into their routine. Let them answer their calls. Even notice by saying, "Wow! You're command central here. You really handle that volume of calls in an incredibly efficient way." Now if there are no calls and they take in one call, don't use flattery that's not based in truth.

Pinpointing Solutions

Solutions solve problems. Plain and simple. That is what we get paid to do as sales professionals.

I had paint on the walls in my house that was there when I bought my house. The can that I found was old, rusted and a brand not sold in my town. I needed to match the wall paint, which is flat latex, to the same color in enamel latex for painting the woodwork, because my eight-year-old daughter wanted the woodwork to be the same color as the walls.

I called the folks over at the local store, and I said, "He-e-e-lp! I've got Sherwin-Williams paint, and it's actually a Glidden color. I know you don't have Glidden or Sherwin-Williams, but can you help me match this color?"

The salesperson said, "Of course we can match that. We're paint problem-solvers. Do it all the time. Perfect matches and no hassles. We've got a computer. Do you have a chip of the paint?" I said, "Yeah, I'll bring the whole can in."

So I came in, and Dave helped me. Dave cut out this little patch of paint from the side of the can and he put it in some spectrometer thingamabobber—and bingo! Five minutes later I'm walking out with the exact same paint I need from a different manufacturer. Problem solved. Imagine if we could meet our customers needs so accurately every time!

How to Present Features and Benefits

I was working with a chemical company, and presented an exercise called "Features and Benefits." To begin the exercise, I handed everybody in the room a clothespin. I said, "OK, everybody, you now work for one of two companies. Half of you work for the Wonderful Wood Company, and the other half of you work for Snap-On Springs."

"I am the owner of the Wechsler Clothespin Company. Your job is to tell me why your wood or your spring would be of benefit to me. I want you to focus your presentation not on features but on benefits."

Everyone in the room looked at me and said, "What do you mean, Warren? What's the difference?" I went on to explain to them the difference between features and benefits

A feature is what something is or what something does. Let's take the example of a clothespin. You might say, "This clothespin is made out of wood, and the wood is sanded." So now we know it is sanded wood. Well, that's a feature—that's what it is or what it does.

I've noticed many, many times working with people in the field that salespeople tend to focus presentations of their company, their products, or their services on the feature—what it is and what it does. And then we make the customer work really hard to figure out what the benefit is. You see, no one buys features, they buy *benefits*. People don't buy a drill bit because of the fluted, pointed, hardened metal, they buy it do make a clean, round hole in their wall or wood without messing up their material.

Let me explain to you what a benefit is. A benefit is why the feature is important—what it means to the person who buys it. For example, if I told you this clothespin is made out of sanded wood, you might say, "That's the feature. What's the benefit?"

The "So What?" Test

"Tell me and I'll forget; show me and I may remember; involve me and I'll understand."—*Chinese proverb*

Now I'm going to give you the real big hint. In order to test whether something you say is a feature or a benefit, you apply the "So what?" test. If you can say "So what?" to someone's claim, then it's not a benefit to you.

Let's go back to the clothespin example. Here's this clothespin. It's made out of sanded wood. What's the benefit to me? So what?

What is the benefit? The benefit is that I will be able to hang my laundry up without getting runs in the fabric, and I don't have to worry about splinters. I can't say, "Oh, so what? I'd rather have bloody fingers or rip all my beautiful cotton, wool, and silk clothing."

Now we have benefits — the benefits of sanded wood are: no splinters (safety), and your clothes won't get ruined (protect your investment). I can't say "So what?" to those things.

Examples of Benefits

Yet salespeople typically spend too much of their time talking about features and not enough time talking about benefits. Benefits will cause people not to say "so what," but to sit up and pay attention to what you're offering. The examples of benefits below will also make the buying decision much easier for your customers.

First, people love to save time. If you can come up with something that will help your customers save time, you have a major benefit to offer. Let's say you are selling accounting services and you have some type of software program that you can install on your client's computer—that's the feature. The benefit is that it's going to save the customer time.

They'll be able to get those reports to you, or the accountant, a lot more quickly. The reports will be accurate, they'll be simple, and the customer will save time. Saving time is a key benefit.

Saving money is another very key benefit. Now saving money doesn't always mean "having the lowest price." It means that your overall solution can help people save money. That is something that they cannot say "So what?" to.

Another thing that people like to buy is something related to the lifestyle they have or desire to have. How can they be safer? How can they have the image they want? How can they keep up with the Joneses? How can they be innovators or leaders within the groups that are important to them?

These are all examples of lifestyle enhancement—image, safety, security—to which people will not be able to say "So what?" Lifestyle enhancement is a key benefit.

When I talk to my clients, I use feature and benefit statements. For example, I might say to a prospect, "I am a sales educator, speaker, and sales coach. I'm a resource to management. I conduct workshops, seminars, keynote speeches, and I have a whole lineup of educational materials that sales professionals can use."

Now, if that were all I said, I would just basically have done all those things I talked about earlier. I "feature, feature, feature, feature, feature" you, without telling you any of the *benefits*.

So what are the accompanying benefits? Well, when I have a chance to work with salespeople, I help them increase their incomes. I help them be more efficient with their time. I help them achieve greater career satisfaction. I help them overcome some of the morale issues that they face as salespeople. I help inspire them to be the best people they possibly can be. I help them find and keep more customers. I help them increase the revenue and profits of the company for whom they're working. These are all examples of corresponding benefits that I talk to people about when I'm mentioning the features of working with my company.

Look at your own company and its products and figure out aspects of your business and solutions that are features, and then convert those into benefit statements. Don't make your customers work so hard to figure out what the benefits are.

Let me give you one more example. I am looking at a timer that's on my desk. One of the features of this timer is that it has three buttons. You might say, "So what?" Why is it important that it have three buttons?"

Actually, the buttons are ergonomically placed so that the timer fits right in the palm of my hand and two of the buttons are right at the place where my thumb and index finger would be. Feature, feature, feature, feature. What's the benefit to me of using this particular timer?

The benefit is that I'm able to time my speech segments more accurately without thinking about it too much. It's easy to use and it's quick, so I'm not going to make mistakes. If I want to time anecdotes while focusing on my gestures, I can watch my form in a mirror, keep my fingers right on the buttons, and be able to record the time without having to look at it.

This allows me to be a more effective self coach because I don't have to focus my energy on looking at the stopwatch. The buttons are placed so well that it's natural for my thumb and index finger to touch them at just the right places.

A salesperson's job is to paint pictures for people, and that's what I've done in the example that I've just given you.

In your business, you know an awful lot about what features and benefits your products or services can offer customers. I suggest that it's time to take out a piece of paper, a pencil, and start writing these things down.

When I started my business in 1987, I remember sitting in the basement of my house in a suburb of Minneapolis, Minnesota, writing out the features of my company and the corresponding benefits. Now you might say, "Why in the world did you, the sales professional, feel compelled to sit down in your basement and write those statements out?" The reason is: "The palest ink is better than the best memory." It's a well-known Chinese proverb.

The point is if you write things down before you go out and see your customers, you will remember what you wrote down. That's why I took the time to write those things out when my business was new.

A Caution Out of the Blue A common sense point to be made is not to be *overeager* with providing solutions for your customer. There are too many times when a prospect says, "I really like blue," and we jump right in and start presenting prematurely. In this case, if the customer says, "Well, you know I work with ABC Company because I really like blue." We jump in and say, "Blue. We wrote the book on blue. We've got navy blue, powder blue, sky blue, royal blue, blue polka dots, blue stripes, and we do blue like nobody has before; we are so blue we could write a song about the blues!"

If you do this, your customers will roll their eyes, emotionally shut down, and stop talking to you. Why? Because they think you are going to try to top everything they say they like.

Here's the proper technique: When people are explaining what their likes are, hold your fire. Make notes to refer to again, but let the customer or prospect keep talking. The customer should be doing 80 percent of the talking; talk only 20 percent of the time, simply to introduce the next topic.

The Salesperson's Paradox

The salesperson's paradox is that your customers expect you to know all kinds of things about your products and services.

Let's go back to the paint example. The sales people know what surface to put it on, how long it takes to dry, how to apply it, at what range of temperatures to apply it. They know what paint works better on metal or wood or new wood or old wood or wrecked-up wood, or blah, blah, blah, blah, blah. Let's just say that you walked into the store and had a very simple question such as, "Should I use a pastel color or a neutral color to paint my deck?"

I just asked for the tip of the iceberg, the barest bit of the knowledge these experts have. The people who practice this craft know so much about paint they could probably give a paint lecture. In fact, they could probably teach a paint course at the local community college.

Now what's the paradox? The paradox is that your customers expect that you're going to have 100 percent of the knowledge on the products and service that you sell, but on any given day, with any given customer, you need probably 1, 2, maybe a maximum of 3 percent of that overall knowledge.

The issue for salespeople is that when the customer comes in and asks an "eyedropper" question such as, "Would it be better for me to use the pastel or a neutral color of paint to cover my deck?" we in the sales profession open up the fire hose. We soak them with information, and pretty soon they are so confused they don't know what is happening.

In order to make the paradox your friend and not your enemy, remember that when people ask you very small questions you should respond with very small answers.

The Misconception of "Overcoming" Objections

"When we accept tough jobs as a challenge and wade into them with joy and enthusiasm, miracles can happen."—*Arland Gilbert*

This is another area where I am a maverick in terms of sales education. There are a lot of books written and seminars that are focused on how to anticipate and overcome objections. The image this conveys for me is a boxing match in which I, the salesperson, am trying to knock out the customer and to get them flat on their backs. When I win they lose, or when I win, they're unconscious. It's a completely absurd thought. In sales we are trying to create a situation that is good for both parties. So instead of thinking in terms of overcoming anything, think in terms of being collaborative and collegial.

Work with customers to help them understand, identify, and overcome any areas of concern or resistance they might have. We are both on the same side of the table, working on the same issues for the common good; salespeople no longer serve as partisan advocates. Let's forget about overcoming anyone's resistance and instead work with our customers to understand what's going on.

ASK THE SALES DOCTOR

PEOPLE WHO WANT "DEALS"

Dean writes from Minneapolis: "I have a lot of trouble in the business I am in with people wanting "deals." They feel that if they are not getting a "deal," they are not getting what the other guy is getting.

> *"Quality remains long after the price is forgotten."*
> *—Edward C. Simmons*

Do I have to set up a pricing structure in which I'm charging more to make these deals? Is there a way around the guy who always wants a deal? Am I just not making him feel "special" enough already?

ANSWER

First, you have to ask yourself some tough questions. In other words, are you presenting yourself as a "dealing" kind of guy? Are you presenting yourself as someone who will cut the price by 5 percent when you think someone's not going to buy today?

What I'm getting at is, do you really believe in your pricing and your value? Are you willing to walk away from business if somebody won't buy at what you feel is your fair price?

Also, do you have published pricing with a discount schedule for volume? For example, if you're in radio or print advertising, there is a published rate. The published rate lists the cost for one insertion in print or one time on the radio.

It also lists the cost for twelve insertions. If you're in every month with a half-page, here's the rate. If you're on the radio three times a day at drive time and you commit to a month at a time, you get volume discounting.

If people are looking for the "deal," do you have a published schedule you can work from and show people that if they use less of your product or service, the price has to be higher?

Here's something else to think about. Have you given "deals" in the past? Do you personally have a reputation for "deal-making"? "Oh, well, when Dean comes by, if I just hold out long enough, he'll start knocking something off, so I can get a better deal."

Now on to the answer you asked for, Dean. It's no. Everybody doesn't want a deal.

Everybody wants value. I'll say it again: "Everybody wants value." It is true that some people like to dicker, so if you have to build flexibility into your pricing for them, that's fine, as long as you're consistent within your value proposition.

If a customer insists on a discount and you want to stand firm on your price, say, "Look, I'm giving you a great value. Here's why, and here's the benefit to you". Sometimes that person is just trying to see if you'll negotiate on your pricing. If you won't, they actually respect you more because they think, "Here's somebody who really believes in his price, and I'm going to buy into that as well."

But let's just say you have to give away something on price for those people who want to feel that they're getting a deal. Number one, if you have a published pricing schedule, give away very small concessions. If you have a one-insertion price and a twelve-insertion price, and the person wants three insertions, don't drop to the twelve-insertion price. Don't give everything away at once.

Also, if you're at $100 per issue and somebody wants to offer you $50, don't just rush to the middle and split the difference. Don't just say, "OK, $75 a month." Start a lot higher than that. Finally, don't give it to them right away. Ask them if they will buy. Say to them, "Look, I'm offering you $100. You want $50. If I gave you $92 today, would you buy?"

So you get the commitment from them before you even say that they've got the discount. You're making clear, "If I did this, would you do that?" You want to separate the serious buyers from the "shoppers", the people who are just buying on price.

So as far as the pricing goes, don't split the difference, don't give it away all at once, and don't give it in even increments. If you're at $100 and they're at $50, and you give $90, then $80, they think maybe they'll get $70, and then $60. Make that increment smaller and smaller as you get closer to your bottom line.

You have to know when enough is enough. Once you establish your bottom line, move up from there, and add that value to every call you make. You'll be amazed at how many fewer people are going to think they're dealing with the "Deal-a-Day Company."

Having Empathy To understand why customers slow down the sales process or prefer not to move forward, we have to understand why they feel or think the way they do.

> "People don't care what you know until they know you care."—*Robert K. Huff*

It's not about us, it's all about them. It's all about empathy. Empathy means that we understand how someone else feels, although we don't necessarily feel the same way he or she does. It means understanding what is said, understanding what is felt, or seeing that point of view.

These are examples of letting the customer know that you *acknowledge* that he has a feeling or a thought and that you are empathizing.

Empathy is different from sympathy. Sympathetic salespeople fail. Sympathy means "I feel the same way that you do." It gets us emotionally involved in the customer's area of concern; we feel like she does and we lose the moment to help her work through resistance or concern. If he says that the price is too high, and we sympathize and remember a similar situation when we were considering a purchase, we won't be able to help our customer or prospect and will not be able to work through their concerns effectively.

Let's say you went to a sympathetic doctor to help you with a knee problem. Now the doctor doesn't know that you have a knee problem, you just walk in and say, "Doctor, I'm hurting," and instead of asking us what's wrong, she says "Oh, well, when I was on the ski slopes in Aspen last weekend I injured my ankle. Now I can't go to ski this weekend. I'm just feeling so bad about that."

The sympathetic doctor feels the same way we do, but does not convey an understanding that you are in pain. You'd never go to a sympathetic doctor. Imagine on the other hand if you went to an empathetic doctor. You walk in with a problem. The doctor says, "What's going on? How can I help you? When did it happen? Where's the pain? Is it throbbing, shooting? Does it come and go? Is it constant? Does it hurt when I do that? How about when I do this? What would you like the end result to be?"

These are all ways for the empathetic doctor to help us move through our areas of concern, move through our pain, and get to a solution. This is what I mean by throwing out the concept of over-coming objections and instead working with our customers. Let me show you exactly how to do this.

1. You empathize.
2. You always restate their area of concern in your own words: "I understand that you're having a problem with the way our product is packed fifty to a box and the way you're buying it

now is twenty-five to a box." So now you have restated their area of concern.

3. Now you talk about the implications. "What does that mean to you in your business?" Get them to show you the implications. "What is it about the way you're buying twenty-five to a box that is meaningful for you?" Then they explain. You say, "I understand that. Let me ask you a question." Now you present why your product is packed fifty to a box—maybe there's a cost savings, or maybe there's a handling issue that goes away. So you ask the customer to see it a new way. This is an example of understanding the implications, presenting how your product or service might be able to work with their area of concern, and showing them how it could be OK for them to move forward in spite of any concerns.

4. The final part is to confirm that you've moved beyond the objection, or helped them understand, or helped them work through that initial resistance, and you're both ready to move forward in the sales process.

ASK THE SALES DOCTOR

QUESTION

Samuel sent this email to the Sales Doctor (warren@ totalselling.com): "Sometimes I work with potential customers and I can't get them to open up and talk to me. Why is this?"

ANSWER

Most of the time, it is because even though we think we're asking great questions, we're really not. We are focused too much on closed questions, that is, questions that demand a yes or no answer. Like; "Do you buy from Smith Supply?"

Yes. "Have you been buying there for a long time?" No. With only these types of questions we don't get much information. When we start asking open ended questions we learn more. "From whom do you buy now?" "How long has that relationship been going on?" "What is about Smith Brothers that keeps you gong back?" The difference between open and closed is one of the reasons why people don't open up as much as we'd like. In my experience in working with sales people, I am amazed at how many times either the salesperson is talking too much or asking too many closed questions. Try asking more open ended questions and you will see that people open up to you a lot better.

Asking For the Commitment

Asking for the commitment is the most important phase of the sales process. I have had personal experience in being a "professional visitor." A professional visitor is someone who is very good at the previous phases of the sales process, as I've described them, yet will never simply come out and ask for the order, ask for the commitment, or ask the customer to move to the next step.

This is really the difference between being average in sales and being exceptional in sales. You know what? It's not about closing. You can't *close* a sale.

Let me repeat that. You cannot close a sale. Too many salespeople have read books on how to close a sale, with titles like *The Academy of Closing*, *The Secrets of Closing*, *The Top Closers*, or other nonsense like that.

The best salespeople are people who understand that *at the end of the presentation there is a transition to make into the next step*. And it's not closing. It's a very similar idea, yet in a very subtle and powerful way it's completely different. The last phase of the sales process is to simply ask for a commitment.

In some cases this means asking for additional meetings or information, or asking for the customer to commit to give us more time. In other cases it means asking the customer to let us compete for a piece of that business that we know is out there.

ASK THE SALES DOCTOR

QUESTION

Here's a question from Carlotta: "I don't get it, Warren. All the books I've read tell me I have to be a strong closer— and you tell me that that's a fallacy, that I don't have to close at all. If I can't close the sale, how am I going to earn my way in the straight commission business that I'm in?"

ANSWER

There is a very subtle difference between the phrase "closing the sale" and the phrase "ask for the sale." What I'm suggesting is that the customer decides whether they are going to buy or not buy. Our job is to simply ask the question, to ask the obligating question. We certainly want customers to make decisions to move in our direction. That is, to buy products and services from us. However, doing so is not based on manipulative closes that we learn by heart and present to our customer in a way that we position ourselves to win regardless of whether the customer wins. Yes, we have to bring the business in the door, yet the way we do that is by asking the customer to buy, not by trying to close the customer. It's a very interesting distinction. We don't close. The customer decides whether they are going to buy or not buy.

The Obligating Question

"Lack of will power has caused more failure than lack of intelligence or ability."—*Flower A. Newhouse*

Every time we are in this position, it's up to us to ask what is called an "obligating question." Ask an obligating question. What I mean by this is a simple question that can be asked very easily. For example:

Is there anything stopping us from moving forward?
When can we get together next to fill out the details on how we can work together?
Would you like to take delivery on Tuesday?
Who else needs to be involved in the decision?
Are you excited about moving forward?
Would you like to start with a full carton or a partial carton?

These are obligating questions because they ask the customer or prospect to make a response that lets us know if they're moving forward, if they're moving backward, or if they are not moving anywhere, or if they're going to raise some issue—an obstacle, resistance, or a delay.

Let's talk about the technique or the tactics of what obligating questions are all about. The reason that the obligating question is so difficult to ask is that we are afraid that we might get a response that we don't want. Obviously, the response we want is yes, yet sometimes the response is maybe, which may mean "I don't know," "I'm not sure, let me think about it," "Let me get back to you," or "Let me talk it over with so and so." It just tells us that the customer isn't in the position to make a decision. Or, the person might come right out and say no.

Now, imagine some of the longer sales cycles in which we may have invested one or more years in getting to this point. If one of the potential outcomes might be no, it's not surprising that salespeople are reticent about asking the obligating question.

The only way I've ever been able to overcome this is to think about it in terms of what I can control and cannot control. We can control asking the obligating question. We cannot control the outcome.

It's up to the customer or prospect to decide if he or she is going to buy from us that day, that week, that month, or that year. Our job is to be completely neutral as to the outcome of the obligating question. This doesn't mean that we don't care if the customer buys from us. Obviously, we very much believe in ourselves, our company, our products, and our services; if the customer ultimately decides to go somewhere else, we think that they're making a huge mistake.

We have to put aside whether the customer is going to say yes, no, or maybe *and ask the question anyway*. This is the absolute essence of being successful in sales—to be willing to ask obligating questions at any time during the sales process, not only at the end.

This is a new idea in selling. Yes, the final phase of the sales process is asking for the commitment, yet we have to be in the mindset of asking obligating questions throughout the sales process. We can ask obligating questions when we're looking to qualify our prospects, to make sure that they're a good fit. We can ask obligating questions when we are trying to arrange appointments with our prospects or customers, when we're trying to identify needs, when we're trying to confirm that our product fits their needs, and so on.

There are so many opportunities during the sales process to ask obligating or commitment questions. As I said earlier, this is the absolute distinction between salespeople who are average and salespeople who are exceptional.

Obligating Questions as Selling Advantage

I'll never forget when one of my early sales managers took me into his office. I wasn't doing as well as I possibly could. He sat me down, and he said, "You know, Warren, you're not really a professional salesperson yet." I was shocked to hear that, of course, because I thought I was doing a pretty good job, even though it hadn't been reflected in my sales numbers yet. He looked at me right in the eyes, and he said, "You're a professional visitor. A professional visitor."

A professional visitor is someone who goes through all the right steps in the sales process. They're easy to talk to; they share information well; they don't interrupt the client or prospect when they're talking; they're invited back to make additional presentations. But at the end of the day when they come back to the office, they come back without the commitment or without the order.

> **"Failure is the opportunity to begin again, more intelligently."—Henry Ford**

The sales manager said, "In order to become a professional salesperson, you need to learn to ask obligating questions." And then he put me on the spot. "Give me an example of an obligating question that you used at the last sales interview."

I was stunned. I realized that I had not asked the customer or the prospect to do something. And that's the secret to understanding what obligating questions are all about. And you know why I was afraid to ask that question? It's because of this one small word that begins with "n" and ends with "o." It's called "no." Nobody likes to hear no; in fact most people don't even like to say no.

So here you are; you're a professional salesperson. You get done presenting your product or your service, and there is a time when it's appropriate to say something like, Where do we go from here? How are we doing so far? Would you like to get started right away? These are all examples of obligating questions.

But somehow, because we're afraid of that small word called no, we stay stuck in presenting our solution—we start talking more about features and benefits. Oh, just last week John Smith bought this product and he loved it. And you're going to like too. In fact, Bob Brown bought it two weeks ago.

And we go on and on, hoping that the person is going to interrupt us and say, "Can I buy that?" Or they'll bring out a piece of paper and they'll say, "Can I create a contract here on my desk?" Obviously, it doesn't work that way. But that's what happens to us when we get stuck presenting and are not willing to ask the obligatory question.

Here's the way I figured how to move beyond staying stuck. I thought about some of my heroes, and my hero growing up was a baseball player named Roberto Clemente. He played for the Pittsburgh Pirates. He was in the Hall of Fame; he had made three thousand hits. He was one of the best players in the 1960s and early 1970s. He batted .317 for his career, which meant that almost 70 percent of the time, when he got up to the plate he made an out. He struck out; he hit a fly ball; he hit a ground out; he hit into double plays. He basically failed 70 percent of the time. What was his reward for failing 70 percent of the time? He got into the Hall of Fame. OK, I thought, if Roberto Clemente can fail 70 percent of the time, and he was amazingly successful, imagine what it would be like for me if I only failed 70 percent of the time. Heck, I'd be in the Salesperson's Hall of Fame, wouldn't I?

I began to understand I should always ask the obligating question, but never predict the response. Similarly in baseball, you don't know if you're going to make a hit or an out, but you cannot choose not to go stand in the batter's box. Imagine if Roberto Clemente made eight outs in a row, and then his name was penciled in the lineup and Danny Murtaugh, the manager, said, "OK, Clemente, you're up." And he said, "Oh, no, I failed the last seven or eight times. I'm not going up there again." I mean, it's laughable. He went up there and took his swings. Learning how to ask obligating questions is like taking your swings.

Another way you can look at this situation is to think about the word "no" as "KNOW." In other words, your customers just don't know enough to say yes. Or they don't know enough to move forward. Or they haven't heard enough of the reasons why they might want to get involved with my product or service.

Once you learn how to use the word "know" in your consciousness instead of no, then you'll be able to ask obligating questions.

The Power of Silence   There are very few absolutes in selling, but this is one of them. And that is every time you ask an obligating question, be silent.

Sometimes people are going to be uncomfortable. And that's OK because every time an obligating question is posed a buyer must decide in his or her mind, Is this something I want to do? Do I want this particular real estate space? Do I want to hire this person to be the speaker at my national conference? Is this the type of furniture that's going to fit in my house? Is this the type of automobile I want to buy for myself and my family?

In that silence there's something that happens to everybody. Any buyer, when faced with a decision, goes temporarily insane. It happens to all of us. We all go a little bit daffy. And the reason that it's important for the salesperson to not talk after the obligating question is asked is because it gives the buyer or the prospect or the client a chance to think about what it would be like to own that product or service, or to move forward along the sales process.

Don't be afraid of silence; don't be uncomfortable with it. And you know what? It's not manipulation either. There's an old saying in the sales business: ask for the order and then shut up, because the first person who talks loses.

That's not what we're talking about here. We're talking about the right strategy. Ask an obligating question and then be silent, but not because you're trying to create a win/lose situation. What you're trying to do is allow the other person to think about the question that was asked and then make a decision: either yes, they're going to move forward; or no they're not. Most salespeople become frustrated when there is no decision.

It's not the yes. We love yes. It's not the no. We can learn to love no. It's those maybes. "I don't know. Let me think about it. Let me get back to you." And that is what we are trying to avoid. And the reason that we practice silence is to allow the customer to make a decision.

One final point about asking obligating questions, and this is an advanced technique. And that is (it's another psychological point) if we learn how to be neutral as to the outcome of every question, we will become very strong obligating question-askers. Let me repeat that. If we learn how to become neutral as to the outcome of every obligating question, we will learn to become excellent obligating question-askers—because, as I explained before, you can't close a sale. You can't control the outcome. But you can control your ability to ask the question.

If you take this idea of obligating questions and use it in your sales business, you will be amazed. You can increase your sales by 20, 30, 40 percent. One person told me that his sales, once he understood this concept, increased by 70 percent in one quarter. You can see the power of learning how to use obligating questions as a selling advantage in your business.

Remember, If We Don't Ask, We Don't Receive

So many times we as salespeople are in the position to ask people to make commitments. We ask them to move forward, where we go next to make a buying decision, and to tell us about the next steps. In my experience, the more you ask the more you get.

Conversely, if you don't ask, you don't get.

Or as Wayne Gretsky said, "You miss 100 percent of the shots you don't take."

Chapter Four

Keeping and Growing Your Business

There is an adage in sales that salespeople will promise anything—in other words, they overpromise and then underdeliver. This is absolutely not what professional salespeople stand for. Professional salespeople recognize that the relationship really begins when the customer says yes and establishes a bond with you. Every time a customer says yes, you are earning the right to that business over and over and over again.

Keeping Customers

Let's talk about how to keep customers—not how to find them, not how to get them, but how to keep them. I'm going to share with you exactly how to create excellence in your business so that you are known as a great company that gives great customer service.

Three Attributes

If you don't take care of your customers, two things will happen. Number one: somebody else will. Number two: they will tell anybody who is within earshot about the negative experience that they had with you. Generally speaking, if disgruntled customers had a bad experience with your business, if something didn't go the right way, if they felt that people were rude or weren't acknowledging them or didn't take care of their needs, they will tell between nine and twenty people about their experience. Or if they're like me, when I have access to a microphone, I can tell thousands of people at a time. It's quite simple to avoid this misfortune.

In my experience, customers want simple courtesy, common sense and accountability from us.

Be There

Let's say you go into the bank and somebody is working on reconciling checks and doing paperwork. You're standing there patiently just waiting to be served. How are you going to feel if that person thinks the paperwork is more important than you? You're not going to feel that good about that experience. What are we saying? Over 90 percent of the time, being good in sales is simply a matter of being there when people need you.

Woody Allen always played the same character—that kind of nerdy, neurotic, New York liberal who is always in his head. In one particular movie, *Play It Again Sam*, he says to the character played by Diane Keaton, "I've figured out the secret to being successful in life." She looks at him as if to say you can't even tie your shoes, what do you know about the secret to being successful in life? Woody Allen utters the following most amazing words: "Eighty percent of being successful in life is showing up."

What's the best way to take care of our customers? I've asked customers this question hundreds of times and the most common response is: "Be there when I need you." What this means is that you don't have to be the quickest, you don't have to be the cheapest, and you don't have to be the smartest; but if you are there, if you show up, you'll satisfy your customers time after time.

If you're there when your customers need you, you will be successful. It's not rocket science. It's very simple, common sense. For example, if a customer calls us at 2:00 PM and expects to have a delivery by 10:00 the next morning and you say that you will arrange it, you must follow through on that commitment. Make sure that you know beforehand you will not upset everyone else in your company by making that promise, and it's something on which you can actually deliver.

How about living out this promise by adopting a philosophy that says I'm here for you? Say to those who buy from you, "You're my customer and I'm here for you. Here's my cell phone number and email address. Here's my pager number. Here's a twenty-four-hour toll-free number. Here's my Web address so you can get information even when I am sleeping." How about making sure that your customers know how to reach you, making sure they know who else is on your team, and making sure they know where they should turn when they have questions, problems, or complaints?

Look at how successful FedEx has become. When you absolutely, positively have to have something now, they can get it to you the next day. That was unheard of in the logistics business until they invented the concept.

"Yes, customer, I'm here for you." It's more than just a good advertising slogan.

Be Thankful

What's another great way to take care of your customers? How about saying thank you? Thank you for being my customer. Thanks for placing that order with me. Thanks for giving me the opportunity to continue to earn your business. Thanks for making sure that that paperwork got out on time. Thanks for sending me that information.

Think about all the things you've bought and how few times anyone has said thank you. Thank you for being a customer. Thank you for buying a house through me. Thank you for placing your insurance through me. Thanks for advertising on my radio station.

Thank you. Thank you. Thank you. These are the two most underutilized words in any person's vocabulary, in business or personal life. Use them to endear yourself to your customers. There are so many different things we can thank our customers for. We should never take our customers for granted.

Be Accountable

A final point about keeping customers: Take responsibility for them. Also say to them, "I'm responsible for you"—meaning that, if something goes wrong, the buck stops with you. Don't say, "Oh, if it weren't for those customers I could get my work done." You've heard that before. It's not true. If it weren't for those customers, we'd be out of business.

A common sense component of being accountable is delivering on-time. If you say you can name that tune in five notes, you've now set an expectation of your customer and they want you to be able to name that tune in five notes. So if you name that tune in eight notes, ten notes, or fifty-two notes, you've basically disappointed your customer. Take responsibility and be accountable for your promises.

The Two Most Important Questions We Can Ask Our Customers

As we found in our earlier conversation about prospective customers, it's important to understand that the current customer is your best customer. I have found that most sales organizations can grow their business by 5 to 10 percent every year by simply asking their customers two simple questions.

What Else?   The first question is: "What else can I do for you?" We know that our marketing departments send out fancy brochures and catalogs, advertise on TV, radio, and the Internet—yet when it comes right down to it, buyers have a very narrow understanding of what it is their provider actually sells.

For example, let's say you were in the office supply business and one of your customers bought everything electronic from you—calculators, computers, printers, and peripherals—but your major business was in pens, pencils, and legal pads. Your customer may not see you as a stationery supplier but as a high-tech supplier. They might not even know that you were in the stationery business because it's just not part of their awareness.

Our job is to constantly, consistently, and persistently present other ways that our customers can do business with us, so that we're always in position to be the go-to supplier for anything they could possibly buy from our company. The add-on and the cross-sell are underutilized components of the salesperson's tool kit that should not be overlooked. The questions the follow are all examples of the "what else?" question:

What else can I do for you?
What other products should I be showing you?
What services would you like me to provide to you?
What is on your mind in terms of ways that I can help you, problems to be solved, or concerns you have about other areas of your business?

Who Else? The second question we can ask our customer is "Who else?" We always want to expand our influence within our customer base so that we establish additional relationships with people in the company who can buy. Doing so, we protect ourselves from our competitors who are calling at other levels of the organization.

You can do this without alienating the current customer contact. You can say, "Who should we be approaching at your company in addition to you?" or, "Who else besides you might we connect with here at your company?" In a typical company there are multiple types of people we could be calling on, and it's important for us to know who else we should be working with. It's a great way to get an internal referral.

ASK THE SALES DOCTOR

QUESTION

Felix wrote in from Mexico City: "I've heard all these stories about asking for referrals, but I've tried it and it doesn't work. Why are you so sure referral requests actually work?"

> "Just keep going. Everybody gets better if they keep at it." —Ted Williams

ANSWER

I think the reason that referral requests work is that the people who are successful are doing it in the right way. The reason that the referral is not a generally well-utilized tool is that we are not specific enough when we are asking the referral source. If you simply say, "Do you know somebody who is looking for a new office equipment supplier?" your referral source can't think quickly enough because you're not giving enough information. She is looking into her own mental Rolodex and seeing a sea of faces, names, companies and logos floating in front of her mind.

A better way would be to ask, "Who do you know who is involved in purchasing decisions in banks, financial institutions, architectural firms, accounting firms, engineering firms, and any other professional firms that seem to move a lot of paper as opposed to manufacturing or distribution? This is an area that I'm really focused on and I'm wondering if you could give me resources that work within those industries?"

In fact, you might say, "Here's a list of companies I'm looking to reach. Do you know anyone at these companies?" Now you can see that difference. Once you put a specific type of customer or specific company name in front of people you'll be amazed at how well connected they are and how many referrals they can actually give you.

New Technology

It almost goes without saying that using new technology is a fantastic way to go about expanding your business and keeping customers. There are new technologies pioneered every day that are going to be helpful to you as a salesperson. It doesn't matter if you're reading this book five or fifty years from the time it was written—new technologies and new ideas will be there to help us move forward. It's a shame, though, as many salespeople are afraid to embrace new technology. Instead, they get stuck in a rut and just do what they've always done.

Over the years, many new technologies have come along to help salespeople. In the late 1970s and early 1980s, the cellular phone was a new innovation. Back then it was called a "mobile phone" or a "car phone" because you had to hardwire it into your car. I knew a lot of progressive salespeople who put those devices in their cars when the phones cost twenty or thirty times more than they do now. Why did they pay so much for mobile phones? Because they knew the technology could save them time and help them keep in touch with their customer base—and they didn't have to pull off to the side of the road to use pay phones all the time. Progressive salespeople embrace new technology.

What about the advent of the personal computer? Until 1983 there was no such thing as a personal computer, and by the year

1993 they were multiplying like rabbits. Imagine the power of now having huge databases and access to information on a laptop that you can take with you into your customers' office.

Moving forward, we saw the advent of email and the World Wide Web. This is technology that smart and progressive salespeople embrace. For example, I was very impressed by several e-newsletters that came to me. I decided that this would be a great way for me to keep in touch with my clients. I couldn't pick up the phone and call every client every day. I couldn't even call all my clients once a week or once a month, and many times I would leave a message because they weren't there anyway. An e-newsletter enables you to send something of value out to your customer base that they can either open when they receive it, put aside for viewing later, or delete if they wish.

I decided that I would send an e-newsletter every two to three weeks to my customer base. It would be very simple, easy to read, and would encourage them to call me or respond via email if they wanted more information. Every time I send an e-newsletter it generates five to ten new opportunities for my business. Many of these come from my current customers, but many come from people whose email addresses I've gathered over the years at programs I've given or who've come to my website and requested my e-newsletter.

Professional salespeople must embrace new technology and be willing to be the person who will take a risk. Salespeople have the opportunity to become calculated risk-takers. This doesn't mean that we bet the farm on the next roll of the dice, but it does mean that we're willing to try new things. So many times we're doing the same thing over and over again and expecting different results. The salesperson who's moving forward is looking to try new things to move his or her business forward. There is a tremendous need for all of us to embrace change, and many of the new technologies that present themselves are ways for us to embrace changes in the market place, in the environment, and in business.

Technological Use   A powerful technology, as I am writing this book, is using email to communicate and using the Web to promote our business. The interesting thing about email is that we can have a "real time" conversation with our customers and prospects, while not actually having it in real time. By that I mean, if we pick up the phone, call someone, and they aren't in, we have to leave a message. When they call us back and we can't take the call because we're on the road, that's called telephone tag—you never have a chance to really connect the message with why you are calling that person. With email, however, we can send our message, it goes into someone else's inbox, and they can read that information at their leisure—in their real time, so to speak—and then send us a response.

Let's say we're on the road and we get back to our office a couple of hours later. We can open up their response and then we reply in our real time. There are so many opportunities for salespeople to use email as a way to communicate with people.

Growing Your Business

"Setting a goal is not the main thing. It is deciding how you will go about achieving it and staying with that plan."—*Tom Landry*

If we were salespeople who could meet our goals every week, month, and year by simply taking orders from our current customers for products that they buy on a regular and periodic basis from us, then we would never have to grow our business in any other way. If we were in the type of business where we could add on to our current clients' volume by natural growth of our current customers, we would never have to put any energy into growing our business either. What I'm saying is that if we could reach our goals, whether they're growth goals large or small, by simply taking care of our current customers and growing the business with them, we would never have to do new business development. It's a fantasy that rarely comes true. For most salespeople, new business development, or growing our business organically, is something we all need to be experts at. In fact, I would venture to say that because of the factors I mention below, growing our business is more important than ever.

Why New Business Is More Important Today Than Ever Before

"One can choose to go back toward safety or forward toward growth. Growth must be chosen again and again; fear must be overcome again and again."
—Abraham Maslow

In my view, there is no one in an organization who is more valued than the people who can find, win, and keep customers. Nobody! And this is more important today than ever before. New Business. It is the most demanding, the most rewarding, and the most sought-after skill that any person or company is looking for.

Why? Let's look at the reasons.

Diminishing Loyalty of Customers   In the old days, customers placed a much higher value on loyalty to their suppliers. Longer term relationships were the norm. Access to information was not as easy as it is today. Technology hadn't been leveraged to the extent that is can be now.

This is not true today. I've been told by many of my clients that long term relationships have vanished into thin air based on many factors—access to the Internet, dynamic and persistent efforts by new vendors to establish relationships, the globalization of markets, the tendency of manufacturers to cannibalize their own distribution networks and sell directly to the end user, vendors getting by on very small perceived price advantages—the list is almost endless. We live in a very fast, transactional time. People are mobile. They move around more often. Companies upsize and downsize at will and rearrange their employees and their responsibilities. Everything is faster. Computers are faster. Athletes are faster. Video games are faster. We like fast video games, fast computers, and the fast resolution of situations. The slower pace of the past is gone.

Hypercompetition   Today, everybody competes with everybody. The days of established channels in the distribution of products and services are gone. Financial institutions buy up accounting firms. Big box retailers with huge buying advantages have attempted to replace mainstream business. Companies attempt to build market share by invading their competitors' territories, product lines, and customer base. Due to the existence of the Internet, inbound and outbound telesales, direct mail, global competition, very large companies and small niche players, competition is fiercer than ever before.

Temporary Competitive Advantage Is the Rule   It used to be that competitive advantages could be developed and exploited for years at a time. Nowadays, if a product or service is shown to have a competitive advantage in the market, competitors will come into that market right away, or within days. It is very difficult to maintain the competitive advantage that might have gotten us the business in the first place.

There was a popular commercial on television recently where a fashion designer is showing her new women's clothing line on the runway in Paris. Amid the glitz and glamour and flashing lights, a lone photographer snaps the "hottest" dress from multiple angles. The scene changes as minutes later, that same photographer is downloading the images to his laptop computer and sending them thousands of miles away to a factory in Asia via the Internet. In moments the images are being manipulated on a computer screen at the factory, specifications are being created and as the commercial ends, a truck backs up to a discount store and hundreds of the same dress are unloaded for sale to the mass market. Far-fetched? Not really.

Shorter Product/Service Life Cycles   Product and service life cycles are shorter than ever been before. In the past, longer product cycles gave the incumbent supplier an edge over new competitors, because it was generally not in the customer's interest to go to the expense of evaluating new vendors on longer running components. The incumbent supplier had an edge—economies of scale made the incumbent more cost effective.

Just in time manufacturing is the rule today, rather than the exception. Specifications change, giving new competitors a chance to start fresh with our customers on new opportunities. The edge of knowing the customer's needs and having the manufacturing, distribution, sourcing and information systems in place vanish. Every potential supplier starts from scratch. As many of the products that we purchase are obsolete as soon as we open the box, customer tastes change like the weather, and short production cycles are the rule; long-term, long-run product cycles are over.

Smaller Target and Segmentation of Markets   We live in the age of specialization. I remember a skit from *Saturday Night Live* years ago where Dan Akroyd had a store that only sold Scotch tape. I remember laughing as one customer after another would enter the store looking for other products. Tape dispensers, masking tape, anything other than Scotch tape. His response to every request was the same. No dispensers, no masking tape, no glue. We sell 3/4-inch by 650-inch rolls of Scotch tape with the dispenser included. Nothing else. People would shake their heads and leave his store laughing, saying what a jerk.

It's not so laughable today. There are stores that only sell batteries. Stores that only sell hot salsa. Just stuffed animal bears. Just magnets. There are companies who only supply a particular type of bearing or a certain electronic component.

Internet In a word, the Internet changed everything. The Internet and the World Wide Web has brought more change to business that any other phenomenon I have seen in over twenty-five years of professional selling. Certainly in the business-to-business market, the Internet and all its ramifications have had a huge impact. Customers can place orders, track orders, look at specifications, have their questions answered, check delivery, and check prices all with the click of a mouse. Information sharing is virtually instantaneous.

There are no more secrets. I placed the entire text of my first book *The Six Steps to Excellence in Selling* online where people could download the content for free. People who advise me thought that I was crazy. People won't buy your book, they said. People will use your knowledge without paying you for it, they said. Nonsense. I thought it was a great idea. I'm willing to give away what my competition charges for.

I don't want to sound smug, but it was the best thing I ever did. Instead of using my website, www.totalselling.com, as a brochure or teaser, I created an information clearing house for professional salespeople. People all over the world have contacted me and many have become clients because they really understood my positions on professional selling and strong desire to be of service to salespeople. They saw the benefits of what I was saying online and wanted more, live and in-person. The Internet gives me access to people and companies all over the world; it's been an amazing part of the success of my business since 1995, when I established a presence on the Internet and launched www.totalselling.com.

ASK THE SALES DOCTOR

COMPETING WITH THE INTERNET

Bradley says, "The Internet is making my life miserable. In the past, I could sell my customers industrial products at 35–38 percent margins. Now my customers, buyers at large corporations, are using the Internet to source my products for 10–15 percent less. I have to match prices or run the risk of losing the business. My expenses are higher than the Internet companies' expenses. I'm spending money on lunches and golf outings, giving education and consulting for free, and now I get beat up on price as a reward. What's up?"

ANSWER:

You're in a really tough position for a number of reasons. I can recommend two strategies, but you're not going to like the first one. That is, you'd better find some new prospects because your model—lunches and golf outings—35-38 percent margins—in industrial products seems a little bit high to me. I've got a lot of industrial customers, and they're operating on 27–28 percent margins, which is right at your 10–15 percent less. So maybe you've had such great relationships with these people over time that they've been paying more and liking it. Well, that's not the way it is today. With the Internet, you're going to face this every single day now and into the future.

But I will give you some ideas on how you might be able to do a better job at not holding onto this business while maintaining price levels. One of my clients owns a custom automobile/van business, which makes vehicles adjustable for handicapped people. There are four or five manufacturers, three of whom compete on price, two of whom compete on value. My client's selling point is value. I was working

with one of the salespeople in his office who was respond-
ing to a prospect in Portland, Oregon, via the phone. The
person was really beating him up on price. I wrote on a piece
of paper for the salesperson to ask, "Why in the world
would you want to buy this vehicle from me?"

I pose the same question to you. Ask your customers
why they buy from you, or why they *would* by from you, or
why they *like* to buy from you. You'd be surprised at the
response. In the above case, the person said, "Your customers love you. You've got on-site service. You stand
behind your products." And the prospect talked himself into
paying more to work with my client.

What I'm getting at is you have to ask people if you are giving them any value. If you're not, then you're in a very tough
position. You're between the proverbial rock and a hard place.

I feel like I'm being hard on you, but the other thing I'd do
is cut out the golf and the lunch bit. Sounds like Willie Loman
in *Death of a Salesman*. If you think that it's jokes, cigars, alco-
hol, golf outings, and lunches that are going to endear your
clients to you, you are about to experience a rude awakening.
Defend that part of your price disadvantage by finding out a
way that your product or service is better. Is it warranties and
guarantees, or is it service? Maybe your teaching and consulting can be bundled. If they just want the price, you'll take away
the education or you'll take away the consulting.

Lower Barrier of Entry Into Markets In all but the most capi-
tal-intensive businesses, the barrier to entry into most markets has
been lowered. The small business owner can complete with the
largest conglomerate. The largest conglomerate can enter business
quickly. Money is generally plentiful. Lenders are willing to take
greater risks. It's easier than ever to become a competitor.

And because there is so much competition in every arena for all companies, more companies that traditionally have done quite well by staying out of *our business* are discovering that they have to enter new markets to grow. The days of protected territories are over. Manufacturers who believe that they can grow their sales by establishing additional channels of distribution in our backyard will do so with absolutely no guilt. The days of "there's plenty of business to go around" are over. This presents an opportunity for many different companies to get involved in our business. Add to this the fact that the public markets are willing to throw much new capital at expanding publicly held companies, and you've got a pretty dangerous mix in terms of different competitors attacking you in your best customers.

For example, one of my clients was involved in the construction rental business in large capital equipment. In order to grow, the client had to expand into a new area. The area selected needed to be involved in the sales and service of smaller tools and consumable items. In any event, I had many clients on the tool side of the business who felt threatened because this large rental company with public money behind it and a national name was all of a sudden moving downstream from the large capital equipment rental business into their bread and butter, which was tools and consumable items. This is a great example of how your protected market is not as protected as you think, and other companies with a lot more capital will see and opportunity and a way to grow their business at your expense

Mergers and Acquisitions of Our Customers Sometimes we lose business through no fault of our own. I can think of numerous times when a large, satisfied client of mine was acquired by a competitor. This happened to me twice in 1998, when my two largest clients were acquired in a period of six weeks. Overnight, I found myself in the position of losing my two largest clients. In those cases, it was simply a matter of the acquirer determining what services were going to be used, and I was working with the acquiree. There are times when merger and acquisition fever takes over our economy as companies are looking to grow their business and convince the investing public that their business is on a positive upswing. In these times, mergers and acquisitions become all the rage.

There's another reason that mergers and acquisitions occur in our economy—because companies can save operating expenses by merging two like companies together. This can be a red flag for those of us providing products and services to companies that are acquisition targets. Because of this, it's always a good idea to focus on our efforts to bring new business in the door; you never know when your best client is going to be acquired, and you will no longer be necessary.

Business Failures and Relocations It easier than ever before for a business to declare bankruptcy. In some faster-moving segments of our economy, it's almost a badge of courage to admit that you've gone belly up once or twice.

This can be a double whammy because not only does the company declare bankruptcy and no longer have the ability to buy from us, we also sometimes find ourselves in the position of holding the bag on what becomes bad debt because we are an usually an unsecured creditor. (As an aside, it's important to beware of the new potential customer who will call you on the phone and ask you no questions, just can't wait to buy, raises no resistance, and has no interest in what type of price you are charging. In these cases, my general advice, is to run away as fast as you can. You're probably just inheriting one of your competitor's credit problems.)

Companies will go out of business. Sometimes it is because they are being made noncompetitive. Sometimes it is because of mismanagement or sometimes just bad luck, with the draw of being in the wrong place at the wrong time. While I feel bad for those companies, I feel worse for those of us selling products and services to them because we lose business and often are left holding the accounts receivable as losses.

It's also very easy to pick up the business and move. This makes it increasingly difficult for the business-to-business salesperson to maintain successful and profitable business. States are competing with each other to have businesses relocate within their borders. Tax incentives fund districts, tax-deferred areas, planned urban developments, you name it—there are so many different ways that municipalities, cities, and states lure business to move from one state to another. Once again, we may do nothing wrong and still lose a large chunk of our business if one of our customers decides to relocate out of our trading area. Even if they still maintain their relationship with our company, we might find ourselves in the need of developing new business because we are restricted geographically and cannot keep writing the business of a company outside of our territory.

ASK THE SALES DOCTOR

QUESTION

Robert, a Dallas recruiter, asks, "I've had a very good career, and over the last five years my sales have been stable and my management tells me that that's not enough. What do you think?"

ANSWER

If we're not getting better, we're falling behind. The fact that you have a stable business that has not grown is a concern to management because, while you're sales have remained flat, the expenses of the company have gone up. That is to say, the lighting, heating, air conditioning, insurance, real estate taxes, and common area building maintenance expenses are all escalating over time. That's why stable or flat sales are much less valuable to most companies over time. So you will need to light the fire and go out there and find some new business.

Environmental Factors Sometimes our business is threatened or declines because of macroeconomic environmental factors. A sudden or unseen drop in consumer confidence, a national tragedy, or a natural disaster can have devastating effects on our business. If we're not focused on new business as a matter on policy, it can be difficult or impossible to recover from an environmental hit to our business.

For all the above reasons, it is critically important for all businesses and all salespeople to master the ability to bring in new business. I've said in my seminars over and over again to tens of thousands of people that if we have stopped the business of looking for new business, we're out of business: we just don't know it yet.

Growing Your Business in a Crisis

"The way I see it, if you want the rainbow, you gotta put up with the rain."—*Dolly Parton*

Many days, all you need to do is to pick up the newspaper to know that many businesses have been hit with events of crisis proportion. Airlines, hotels, retailers, the stock market—you name it, they're in a crisis. There's a tendency to look at all the bad news and say, "It's time to run for the hills."

In my opinion, we and the market always overreact. The market overreacts to both good and bad news. We as human beings overreact on the upside—we go from happiness to euphoria—and we overreact on the downside—we go from unhappiness to depression.

Four Do Not's and Two Do's The bombings of the World Trade Center and the Pentagon in 2001, and the subsequent feeling that we could at any minute be attacked by terrorists, are not the only crises hurting business today. Keep in mind that we do not need a crisis of major proportion to hurt our sales. We can also lose a lot of business by simply offering bad service, making our top five clients our top five nonclients.

Other unfortunate things also happen. As mentioned earlier, clients move away and companies merge or go out of business. No matter what the crisis is, when business slows down, when sales revenue drops, when profits are leaving and expenses are not, you have a crisis in your business. There are four Do Not's to consider when a crisis hits your business:

- Don't panic. (Maintain an even keel. Focus on what still works.)
- Don't change for the sake of change. (Strong changes can capsize your boat.)
- Don't be isolated or alone. (Talk through your situation with a level-headed colleague.)
- Don't be reactive. (A rolling stone gathers no moss.)
  Don't, don't, don't, don't.

There is a bright side, too. Here are two things that can help us get back on track. (Here come the two do's.) The first do is to *be proactive*. If nobody is calling us because they're shell-shocked or depressed, our job is to get on the phone and make the proactive, outbound call. Divide your clients into three categories. The top 10 percent in terms of revenue, loyalty, or however you choose to rank them, are your *A* accounts. The next 20 percent are your *B* accounts. The next 70 percent are your *C* accounts. Spend 70 percent of your time contacting your *A* and *B* accounts.

Call them up. Talk to them. Ask them how they're feeling. Make sure they know that you care about their business. You're calling them just to reconnect with them. You don't even have to ask for any business. Just reconnect with your customers.

If the conditions are right and the topic moves on to business, by all means, talk about current and future opportunities. Seek out referral business, add-on business, or new business. The main idea, the main concept is: be proactive. Make calls.

The second do is *focus on your strengths*. Focus like a laser beam. Figure out what got you to where you are today. Don't go off on esoteric tangents, wondering if you should get into a new business line or offer some new product or service. Go with what got you there. It's called "Going with the horse that brung ya."

Figure out, "What am I strong in? Is it customer service? Is it the way I approach my clients? Is it information- or technology-based?"

This is not the time to be diversifying into unrelated areas. It's time to get back to core competencies. What are you really good at? That's what you ought to be doing - focusing on your strengths.

And because crisis is the time when so many companies and salespeople think that they should be on the sidelines, our job is to be in the game and make the calls to those people who have said no in the past. Call those people who have said:

No, I don't really need that technology.

No, I'm about to leave on vacation.

No, I'm just back from vacation.

No, I don't need any right now.

No, I'm all set with so-and-so.

No, I'm not interested.

No, I'm in a meeting.

No, I'm really busy.

Now is the time to contact all those people who are good prospects for your products and services, the ones who have said no before.

The best accounts we are ever going to open are the ones where we have had four, five, six, or seven different obstacles,

> **"A problem is a chance for you to do your best."**
> —*Duke Ellington*

delays, or resistances. Now is the time to "out-persist" and "out-hustle" your competitors, to make those calls. Make the fifth call on the same company, or five new calls on five new companies. The persistent and consistent prospecting efforts, the outreaches, the customer contacts, the prospect contacts are things that we all need to be doing when in crisis.

Become a Star By Bringing in New Business

"A great deal of talent is lost in this world for the want of a little courage."—*Smith*

We know that business executives and sales managers are constantly asking where that new business is coming from. And you know what? Very few people are experts at ushering new business in the door.

The person who can bring in new business—the rainmaker, the hunter-type person who can go out there and find the food for the tribe—is the most highly valued person in a sales organization. Of course, the individuals who service the business, that deliver on the promises, are certainly important. I'm talking about another level of importance. That person who can face rejection has become, in my opinion, the most-valued individual in a company.

Why? Developing new business is the hardest thing that any salesperson is ever asked to do. Think about it. If you call on a current customer, they're going to remember you; they're probably going to like you. Yes, there are problems; you're going to overcome them. And then you can get to business. How are you today? What else do you need? How's the current product working? Here's a new idea. Those calls are generally easy to make.

But what about the tough calls—the new business calls? We need to set aside a time, figure out how many calls we're going to make, and track our progress. That sounds really simple, but you know what? In this whole area of new business, I can't tell you how many times the people I work with have been victimized by another saying, which I can't claim credit for: The road to hell is paved with good intentions. "Oh, I meant to make those calls. I meant to get on the phone today and make those business calls, bu-u-u-ut...A good customer called and I had to take care of it. A-a-a-nd I had to track down that order, a-a-a-nd I had to get that proposal out, a-a-a-nd I had to look online and check my email."

You get to the end of the day and you realize you've made absolutely zero new business calls. You're going to get rejected at least half the time, maybe eighty percent of the time. Is that something you wake up and say, "Oh yeah, I think I'm going to work the phone for four hours today and just get rejected for three hours and fifty-two minutes." Obviously nobody likes that. What we have to do is schedule the time to make the calls.

One of my favorite clients once said, "You know, Warren, it's simple. You make ten calls before ten o'clock in the morning." Think about that. If you made ten outbound calls every business day before ten o'clock in the morning, your funnel of prospects and your client base would grow so fast it would be almost dizzying in its scope.

If you track your progress and you find out that you make ten dials and only get through to one person, then you need to either adapt what you're saying, or you're not getting through to the decision-maker. Or maybe you're trying at the wrong time of day, or your approach is just not effective. That's why it's so important to make the calls and track your progress. When I work with my

clients, I have them track dials, approaches, decision-makers contacted, and outcome. And just by looking at the stats over a
couple of days, I know exactly where I can help that salesperson
improve.

Networking Successfully

Networking successfully is a skill that anyone can learn. It is one of
the best ways to build your business—whether you are looking to
maintain the customers that you have or find new ones.

The Art of Painless Prospecting

Let's get down to the nitty gritty right away. How do we network
successfully? "First things first" is the first theme. We have to
understand that we have to help other people get what they want
before we can ever expect to get what we want. When you're networking, first find what the other person you're networking with
professionally is looking for and help that person with her business. Open up your network to the other person and see a way you
can be of service to them. In my experience, doing this comes
back tenfold.

SALES IDEA

UTILIZING REFERRAL PROSPECTING TECHNIQUES

Make a list of twenty-five specifically targeted accounts—
industry, geography, employee, or revenue size. Be as specific
as listing companies by name. Laminate the piece of paper.

With list in hand, use a planned approach to ask our best
clients for referrals.

1. Compliment the client or show your appreciation (they will
usually respond in kind):

I really enjoy working with you. We've been working together
for...

2. Transition statement:

Before we complete our meeting today, there is one thing I'd
like to discuss with you.

3. Reason for the request:

Our research shows that our best sources of business come
from people who know us and trust us, and the best way that
we've found to communicate this trust and professionalism
to others is through the introduction and referral from people just like you.

4. Ask for the referral and *be specific*:

I'd like to ask you for a favor. Here is a list of the companies,
industries, and geographies that I'm targeting. Who might
you know at these or similar companies? Thank you for helping me.

**Action: Make your list of 25, laminate it, and use this
approach with your three best customers this week.**

Be Specific   One of the keys to networking successfully is to be
specific. A lot of people try networking and find out that it doesn't
work for them. Why? Because they say something like, "Do you
know anyone who is looking for a good insurance program?" or,
"Do you know anybody who wants to get involved in a new construction project?" The problem is we all have too many names
floating around in our mind. It is said that when we reach adult-
hood, we have two thousand names and faces in our memory. If
someone approaches us and simply asks who we know, our mental
Rolodex spins out of control and our response usually is, "Sorry,
can't think of anybody." It's important for us to be specific. We have

to ask by industry, by geography, by type of company, by revenue size, by company name, even by specific people.

One by One When we're working in large groups and we affiliate together with a lot of people who are looking to build each others' businesses, we have to focus on one person at a time. Don't try and dig up referrals or network with ten people in your group (if you're in a group of ten) all at the same time. Focus on one person for several weeks and see if you can be an advocate for that person's business for those several weeks. Then move on to the next person. Then move on to the next person and so on.

Getting It Together How do we put it all together? By having a plan. As I have said many times "If you don't stand for something, you'll fall for anything." We have to understand what our business is about, and who our best prospects are. We have to be able to articulate what we are looking for and be able to explain it to other people with whom we network. Next, we have to be willing to take the action. We can think it, we can think we should get some referrals, we'd like some referrals, and we want some referrals. Yet in order to make it happen, we have to take action. That's why the concept "be proactive" is such a strong idea. That's why "just do it" resonates with so many people around the world. If we want networking to happen, we have to make it happen. Pick up the phone, make the call, get a lunch appointment with someone you know, start a networking group on your own and get moving.

I'm reminded of a client, one of the Big Six accounting firms, that had a tremendously successful practice. They had such a great track record that many of their clients would hire away the firm's accounting professionals. As it turns out, after a decade or so, there were literally hundreds of this firm's professionals working all over the country in corporate America. To the firm's credit, they understood the genius of this concept.

Once a year, they invited all the alumnae to come back for a big three-day celebration that included continuing education requirements, seminars, and workshops on what was new or hot in their particular line of work. And they also had networking opportunities in the early morning, late afternoon, and evening to allow the people who used to work at the firm to talk to the people that still worked at the firm.

What do you think was the agenda of the people that were still at the firm? Obviously, they wanted to find out what was going on inside these other corporations. Though many of the corporations were still clients, many had other divisions with whom this accounting firm didn't have any relationship. Over time, this networking function became one of the best business-building tools that the accounting firm had.

One year they asked me to come in and do a session on networking – on how to work a room. I had a great time. It turned out to be so well-received that I added it to the repertoire of things that I do for my clients. It's what I call How to Network, or How to Work a Room.

You'd think it would be easy. Doesn't everybody know how to do this? The answer is no.

Get with the Networking Program

In the Go Get 'Em model, networking education is presented like this: "Here's a big room full of people. You know what to say. You know how to approach them. Go get 'em."

In fact, professional salespeople use specific techniques when working a room.

The first distinction is that there is a difference between working a room in a social setting and working a room in a business setting. Let's say that you're invited to your cousin Jolene's wedding and you show up with a box full of business cards, engraved pens, and notepads. You're handing out cards all over the reception.

Jolene's groom, father, uncle, cousin, or brother may toss you out on your ear. It's a social setting, and you really want to underplay this business networking approach.

In a business setting, however, people expect you to network, work the room, schmooze—whatever you want to call it. And it's absolutely appropriate to hand out cards and take advantage of opportunities to work yourself into groups where people are chatting, especially if you've identified people with whom you're looking to contact. Once you've spotted someone with whom you want to make contact, follow the steps I'm about to give you.

Remember, though, that is there is a difference between the social setting and the business setting. That's not to say that if you meet someone in a social setting you don't do any networking at all. The point is that you keep it understated, abbreviated, and light in a social setting, because people are there to have fun and enjoy the moment, not to talk to you about business.

There's another distinction: even within some business settings, it's not appropriate to solicit members for business. I'll give you an example. I've been a member of Rotary groups since 1985. The slogan of Rotary International is "Service Above Self," meaning that you join a Rotary group to be of service to the community at large and to other members.

If someone in your Rotary group is, for example, a banker or an accountant, she is not supposed to approach you as a Rotarian to solicit your business. If you have an accounting question or a banking question, you go to the accountant or the banker in the group and ask them if they would be kind enough to answer your question or consider being of service to you.

There are many other groups that actually encourage people to network and do business with each other. One example is the Chamber of Commerce. You should expect that others attending a Chamber of Commerce function will approach you to explain their products and services. And they will probably ask if it's appropriate for them to call on you or if you'll consider doing business with them.

So, within trade associations or Chambers of Commerce it's expected behavior for the members to solicit each other for business. With the exception of groups that don't allow networking or business-building, most other groups are OK about it.

Now, let's talk about what to do when you go to one of these functions at which it's appropriate to network. The first thing you have to do is prepare yourself. That means that you take three things with you to every business-opportunity meeting.

First, make sure you take your business cards. I can't tell you how many times I go to an event, I talk to someone, I have an interest in what they are providing, but when I ask them for a card, they get flustered because they don't have any. To not have such a standard business tool makes you look very unprofessional.

Needless to say, if you ask me for a card I've got them falling out of every pocket. I've got them in my wallet, I've got them in my day-timer, I keep them in my briefcase, I keep them in my workout bag, I keep them in all my suitcases. It's a very rare occurrence to catch me without a business card.

You also need a pen or pencil and something to write on. A lot of times you'll have a chance to make notes about quick conversations you've had. You can either take out your business card and jot notes on the back of it; or, during a business card exchange, you can take the other person's card and make yourself some quick notes. When I meet someone and we've had a chance to exchange cards, I will stand aside, away from the action, and jot down the date, the event, and something specific about the conversation I had with that person.

The third thing you need to carry with you is some type of paper. If you decide you need some more extensive notes on a conversation, you'll have something to write them on.

Taking your daily planner or PDA with you to a networking

opportunity is optional. In some business-to-business settings, you may have an opportunity to book an appointment with someone when you are networking. If you don't have your daily planner with you, it's hard for you to know when you could book the appointment. You don't want to schedule an appointment at a time you have already committed to someone else.

> **"Don't trust your memory. Write things down."**
> —*Unknown*

Today's PDAs (personal daily organizers) are so small that most of us can tuck them into a purse or shirt pocket. It ought to be rare for us to ever miss opportunities because we don't have our appointment calendar with us.

So, let's review: you take cards, pen, paper, and a PDA.

Now that you're at this event. What the heck are you supposed to do? The first thing you do is think strategically about what's happening at this meeting.

I usually scan the room first. There have been many times when I know certain people over whom I might want to have some influence are going to be at a particular meeting. I search the room to find out where these people are so that I have a chance to work my way over there. I target the types of people I'd like to speak with.

If you're new to a group and you don't really know many people, take advantage of whatever tools are available to you at the event—maybe nametags or a roster of attendees. Or look for specific industry groups, presidents and owners, tall overweight men, or flashy young entrepreneurs. The point is to define who your best prospects are at a meeting, then target your efforts so that you make sure you have a chance to talk to those people.

So the first thing I recommend is to scan the room, then start working your way from small group to small group, talking to strangers. I know that flies in the face of everything you learned when you were growing up, when your parents told you not to talk to strangers, but I say, "Go find strangers and talk to them!"

Most people go to events and look for their "comfort zone." They get to a meeting in which there are two hundred, fifty, or ten people they don't know. And they find someone they know because they want to stay in their "comfort zone". What I'm saying is: "Get out of your comfort zone and go talk to strangers."

You might say, "Warren, how do I do that if I'm looking at a group of three or four people whose nametags or the way they're carrying themselves lead me to believe they're people that I should get to know? What do I do? Do I just barge into their conversation?"

The answer is no. What you do is go to the group and look for the best place to stand.

In other words, they're not locking arms together. There's going to be some gap. There's usually not a symmetrical arrangement in a small group of people talking. You get into that group, on the outside, and just stand there politely smiling.

As people come to know that there's someone standing there, give them some eye contact. Smile at them. Eventually, a particular conversation or a sentence will end. Someone will turn to you and introduce themselves. Or, if they just turn to you and look, you can start by introducing yourself.

I know this sounds really bizarre and bold, but I've been doing it for decades. I just work my way into a group, stand on the fringe, smile politely with my drink or hors d'oeuvre in my hand, and eventually someone acknowledges me and asks me who I am. Or the conversation slows down and I have a chance to interject myself without being too forward. That's how you break into a small group and talk to perfect strangers.

Now, when you're in the group, there's a tendency to talk too much about yourself. Anybody who has heard this show before knows that I stand opposed to that. I like other people to talk about themselves. In this particular setting, you focus your attention on the other people.

You might say:

Tell me about yourself.

What brought you to this group tonight?

What type of work do you do?

Where do you work?

What do you do there?

What are some of the types of products and services that you produce or distribute?

Who are some of your customers?

What are some of the issues that are facing your business?

What do you think of the speaker we just heard?

How's the food here?

What's the weather like?

How are the Cubs going to do this year?

You basically ask them questions that relate to their own self-interest. After they're done talking about what's important to them, what do you think they're going to do? They're going to ask you what you do.

And now you have a chance to tell them who you are, what you do, who you serve, what type of clients you have, or what type of value you provide in the marketplace. So you have chance to tell your story. But the best way to go about that is to have the other person tell their story first.

Let's say you find someone who seems to have a great interest in what you're doing. Should you drop everything, drag them by the arm, and spend the next forty-five minutes monopolizing their conversation? The answer is no.

If you're in a one-on-one situation and you talk to someone who has an interest in what you're talking about, say to him or her, "Hey, this is really great. I'm happy we've had a chance to get to know each other briefly at this event. I'd like to call you sometime and maybe we can get together and talk further about your company and its needs, and how my company (or product or service) might be of benefit to you. Can we schedule some time to meet?"

They're going to say, "Sure." Then you say, "Great. Can we exchange business cards? Here is mine." You offer yours and ask them for one of theirs.

If the other person doesn't have one of his/her cards, that's OK because you've come prepared. You've got your pen and you've got your business cards. So you simply take one of your business cards, turn it over, and write down all his/her information—name, title, company name, address, phone number, email, and website.

After you've done that, you say, "Hey, great. I've really enjoyed meeting you. I'm sure there are other people you'd like to talk to while you're here. Thanks again."

And then off they go, and you work the room to find someone else. This is how we do networking. This is how we work a room.

The keys we talked about are:

- Understanding the distinction between business and social settings
- Taking the right things with you
- Knowing how to open conversations
- Knowing what to say and what not to say
- Seizing your objectives: meet people and gauge their interest. Don't monopolize people's time and take them away from the main reason they're there—the business or social event.

ASK THE SALES DOCTOR

FOLLOWING UP AFTER A NETWORKING EVENT

Greg, a Midwestern banker, asks, "What do you recommend doing after you' ve attended a network party where you met potential customers?"

ANSWER

The first thing I always do after one of those functions is lay out all the cards on a table and prioritize them. I'm looking for priorities as far as how they affect me. Where is the greatest revenue potential? Where is the quickest path to revenue? How loyal is that revenue? What type of name recognition am I going to have if I use that company's name as a satisfied client? What type of referral opportunities would there be if I were to do business with them? Could that be the beginning of a long chain of events that would get me involved with other companies? Those are the criteria I use to prioritize my prospects.

The top 10 of those cards are going to be what I call your *A* prospects. With the *A* prospects, you take out a piece of paper and you write them a handwritten thank-you note. "Dear Joe, I really enjoyed meeting you at the Chamber of Commerce Overtime function. Based on what we talked about, I'm excited about the potential opportunity to work together." Within three or four days of that note being mailed, you call the people up and ask them for the appointment.

With everybody else, all the other people that aren't the As, just wait a week or so, and then call them up in order of priority. If you have the time, follow up with a quick phone call, put them on your mailing list, send them a newsletter, or send some type of marketing their way.

A lot of people attend networking functions and they never follow up. I'm a big believer that if you're going to go and be involved and spend all that time and energy and sometimes money attending some of these events, it's really important to maximize your efforts by following up.

Final Words on Networking

Without focus or effort, networking is not going to happen. The only place that success comes before work is in the dictionary. If you want to be successful at networking, if you want to practice painless prospecting, you have to make the effort. Look over these principles, jot down some notes on what works for you, and go out and do it.

Part Two
Sales Plan

Chapter Five

Developing a Sales Strategy

"People with goals succeed because they know where they're going."—*Earl Nightingale*

Red Motley said in the thirties what is still applicable today. "Nothing happens until someone sells something." It's a deceptively simple, true statement.

Yet it's not that easy. Many people confuse the end result, selling something, with what got them there—a sales process based on a sound sales strategy. In other words, you may sell a product or service very well, but it is usually your plan, not stone-cold luck, that got you that sale in the first place.

Start Here

Do you remember when you played the game Monopoly, whether you played the game as a child or as an adult? The game begins when peo-

---

"He who wills, can."
—*Anonymous*

---

ple select their pieces, get a grub stake of money, and then proceed to march around the board based on the rolls of the dice, collecting properties and charging rent with the goal of monopolizing the real estate market and bankrupting the other players in the game. While we're not necessarily playing monopoly when we're playing the sales game in terms of sales strategy, the analogy is still appropriate. When you play monopoly you know what your goals are. You know what the game plan is, you know what the expectations are, you know where you begin, you know there's a middle, and you know what the end game is. Similarly, sales planning or strategy is a concept that encompasses the same ideas. In order to know where we want to go, we have to know what the goal is. For most of us in sales, it usually is a dollar number: it's the amount of sales we want to generate, the amount of gross profit we want to generate, the dollars and cents of products and services that we'd like to sell in any given time period. You get the idea. We need to put together the pieces, which are our sales process, as we've described before, our sales plan, which we are discussing now, and our sales practice, which we'll cover later. As I've said earlier in the book, if we're able to generate enough business from our current customers in the day-to-day reordering process and grow our business at 10, 12, or 15 percent a year, we really wouldn't need a sales plan. We would just wake up in the morning, see our Monday calls, see our Tuesday calls, see the people we see every other Wednesday—and on the last day of the last month of that calendar year, we would book the exact amount of business we needed in order to hit our goal for the year. Not likely for most of us.

As we all know, as anyone who has been in sales more than thirty minutes knows, this is not the way it works in reality. It is up to each and every one of us as individuals to understand exactly what it is that we're trying to attain in terms of sales dollars (or whatever it is we want to measure). Then we have to know precisely what we are going to do in terms of what actions we're going to take, what customers we're going to serve, what value we're going to provide, and what we're going to exchange in the market place in order to reap the rewards of our efforts. Then we need to commit that plan to writing. So many people think they are going to do something, or dream they are going to do something, or wish or hope they're going to do something, and at the time everything sounds great and we really, really want to achieve that and be successful. Then we get distracted. Some new idea comes to us or some change in the marketplace happens and the dream goes away—it just disappears like bubbles in the bathtub. This is why having a written sales plan we can refer to on a daily basis, weekly, monthly, quarterly, or annual basis is so important for our success.

It is critical to have a *sales strategy* or a *sales plan*. Let's start on a rather general level because there are many questions to answer:

- Who are my best potential customers and why?
- Are manufacturers, distributors, retailers, or service companies the best fit for me?
- What is the size of the companies?
- How many employees do they have?
- What sales revenue do they have?
- What percentage of their overall sales might they spend on our product or service?
- Where are they located geographically?
- What is the level of the decision-maker we're looking for? Is it the president, the owner, the purchasing agent, the person in the field, or the person behind the desk?
- How do we position ourselves for the best chances of success?
- What are our relative strengths and weaknesses compared to our competitors?
- What are threats within the marketplace that will affect me and my company in pursuit of my sales strategy?

- What about our competitors? What are their strengths? Weaknesses? What are their opportunities to penetrate our market? How can we be a threat to them?

In other words, before we even think about making that initial call on that brand new prospect, we should set ourselves up for success, not failure. By understanding our unique positioning—where we're strong and our competitors are weak—we are increasing our chances for success. Having that strategy, having an understanding of where we're going, is non-negotiable for selling success.

There is a saying: "If you don't know where you're going, you'll probably end up in a place you never intended." This is why it is important to have an effective sales plan.

ASK THE SALES DOCTOR

QUESTION

I'm in the personal services business and I really believe that everyone is a prospect. Would you say that is a bad way of identifying prospects?

"Don't confuse activity with productivity."
—B.W. Luscher, Jr.

ANSWER

If you are selling a particular type of universally accepted product like gasoline, and you're in Los Angeles where everyone has a car, you're right—"everyone" might be a prospect for you. It's just better to focus your efforts in a more targeted fashion. Why not do marketing to your current customers who have been buying fuel from you at your corner gas station, and then expand that and say that if you bring a new customer into the store to buy fuel or groceries, you'll give them a five-dollar coupon off their next purchase.

> And then why not target the immediate neighborhood? Why not target the various traffic by-ways and highways where people who live in your bedroom community are commuting into cities and towns that are close by? It just means that when we work smart at identifying our best prospects we could have better results than by taking an approach that is so dispersed in its design.

Begin with Your Current Customers

"Wise men have long said, 'You are what you think.' Program your mind to think positively about your achievements."—*Success Tip*

Why not start with our current customers to get some ideas on who our best prospects might be? We are looking for trends. There is probably a "rhyme or reason" to why we do business with certain types or categories of customers.

Here's how to do it. Write down your top ten customers on the left side of a clean sheet of paper. Now, on the right side of the paper, write down where those customers came from. Now I don't mean they came from Georgia, or they were born in Pittsburgh. I mean, how did that business come your way?

When I ask my customers this question, generally the answers are: a cold call; I inherited the account and I grew it; it was a referral from a current customer; it was a call-in; or it came from a center of influence—someone well-connected. What we look for when we look at those top ten is this: What trends do we see?

Are they all a specific type of organization? Are they large or small companies? In these companies do we have to have access to the highest-level decision-maker? Do we find that most of those customers originated as a call-in that started as a small acorn and grew into a big tree? Can we define patterns that tell us where we should be making initial calls—for example, referral calls?

Let's say we're in an accounting profession, and three of our top ten clients are closely held distributorship companies. What does that tell us? It says that for one reason or another, we've developed an affinity or a good relationship or expertise within closely held distributorship companies within our trading area.

If three of our top ten come from the same type of business, then I'd say, "There might be 12 or 15 or 22 or 118 companies just like that in my trading area that I am not doing business with." We can see how effective it is to have a sound strategy or sales plan.

ASK THE SALES DOCTOR

PRIORITIZING ACCOUNTS USING FIVE CRITERIA

Melanie asks: "Warren, I have inherited a client base of over three hundred accounts in the medical field. I work for a large pharmaceutical company. I can really only effectively service my top fifty, and I'm thinking about prioritizing based on last year's revenue. What do you think?"

> "Prioritize and manage your time so that your first things come first, not last."
> —Success Tip

ANSWER

Congratulations on inheriting a client base or a territory that has 300 accounts. A lot of people who start out in sales or come into a new territory find themselves in either a no-business situation where they have to start from scratch, or a territory where they need 50, 60, or 80 accounts to survive, and they're given 10 or 20. You are in a great position if you've got an account base of 300 and your challenge is to whittle it down to those top 50 or 60.

I would not prioritize those accounts based only on revenue. Here's how to do it. First, I look at my client base in terms of *A*, *B*, and *C*. *A* is the absolute top 10 percent of my client base. The *B* accounts are the next 20 percent, so my *A* and *B* books, represent 30 percent of my overall accounts, in your case, about 90 accounts. And then 70 percent is the *C* book, or the rest of the accounts, in your case about 210 of those 300 accounts.

From a time standpoint, Melanie, you should spend 50 percent of your time with that *A* group of clients. In your case, carve out half of your time to spend with those top 30. Then spend 30 percent of your time with the next 20 percent, so that would be spending 30 percent of your time with the next 60 accounts.

You're spending 80 percent of your time with 30 percent of your client base. Then the balance of your time, the 20 percent, would be spent with the other 70 percent. You might ask why you spend any time at all with the C accounts. It's because you are farming those prospects for next year's *A* and/or *B* accounts.

Now to your real question. I think you should rate your client base in a number of different areas. Here's a method that works famously.

The first criterion is actual or potential revenue. I have a scale that determines if that client is a one, two, three, four, or five. Five is the best score; one is the worst score.
The second category I look at is profitability. You can have great revenue, but if you're not making any money on that account, then it's really not as valued as you think it is. So I rate that particular aspect on a scale of one to five as well.

The next category I use is what I call loyalty. Is this going to be a transactional thing, where I just get one large order and that's it? Or is this something that's going to develop into a long-term relationship? Obviously in your field, I would imagine that you're calling on the same medical doctors, physicians, clinics, and hospitals. They're not just going to buy a whole batch of pharmaceuticals from you once and never come back. So maybe that's not as important an issue in your business. I'm just showing you by my own example what those criteria are that I use. The third criteria I measure is loyalty on a scale of one to five.

Then I measure fit. Based on what I sell and what my customers buy, are the interests aligned perfectly, somewhat, kind of, or not at all? I look for the best possible fit and rate the customer accordingly.

The final criterion is that people are generally going to follow the leader, so name recognition becomes important. I look at my client base and ask if each client has good name recognition in the field. If I aimed my efforts at developing this client into an *A* account and someone asked me who I work with—would that client be a great account to be able to mention by name? It's what I call name recognition, and that's my fifth criterion.

There's a total potential of 25 points. A company with 20 or more points is an *A*. Any account that has 15–19 points is a *B*. Below that is a *C*. Now focus your energy on the *As* and the *Bs*.

Targeted Prospects

"Life is like riding a bicycle. You don't fall off unless you stop pedaling."—*Claude Pepper*

Focusing our energy on selected focused prospects is called "targeted prospecting." We might say to ourselves, based on our research into our current client base, "I know I could be good at selling to more high-tech companies that need additional staffing." So now you might say, "What companies need that type of high-tech staffing?" Then we put together a list of targeted accounts.

Setting up targeted accounts, looking at our current customers, and seeing trends and patterns helps us reduce that rejection we're going to face on those initial calls. If we can increase the initial acceptance of our approach from three or four positive responses out of a hundred to be maybe eight, ten, or twelve, we've just increased our effectiveness by 300 percent. That's what good salespeople look for—increasing the success rate incrementally.

Look, none of us want to go out there to face no every single day, calling all these people who are going to say, "No, no, no, no, no, no, no." Anything we can do to improve our odds is going to be great, especially when we know we are increasing our chances of success strategically.

Sales Idea

Create a Top Ten Advocate System

"Nothing too high for a man to reach, but he must climb with care and confidence."

—*Hans Andersen*

Centers of Influence (COI) and Very Important People (VIP) can be terrific sources of referrals for professional sales people. They are well-connected, well-respected, and have a reputation they are willing to help others. Referred prospects are more likely to grant an initial face to face meeting than a non referred prospect.

Examples of COI and VIP include people in the following fields:

- venture capitalists
- insurance companies
- bankers
- accountants
- corporate executives
- board of directors members
- attorneys
- well-connected businesspeople and entrepreneurs
- people with whom we have a personal relationship that is not business-related (from children's activities; social and civic organizations; salons; people from whom we buy products; contacts religious groups, fitness centers, and clubs)
- clients (current, inactive, previous, lost)
- associates within our own business

In order for us to strengthen the relationship with COIs and VIPs, it is up to us to be proactive. Commit to monthly contact with each one—email, phone, personal visits, letters, breakfast meetings, invitations to events—and make sure that our message on what we are able to offer our clients and prospects is regularly and consistently communicated.

Action: Create a Top Ten Advocate List and make at least one contact to a CIO or VIP's on your list monthly.

Why a Plan is So Important

In my experience working with a large distributor in the Midwest, I found that they had over three thousand accounts on their books that they were attempting to cover with fifteen salespeople. In this distributor's industry, it was urgent that one of their salespeople appeared at the door when the customer was ready to place an order. When you do the math, you start to realize that fifteen sales-people trying to each cover two hundred accounts in an adequate manner is basically unattainable.

I suggested that we reduce the amount of customers we called on by over 50 percent. This was a shocking concept to the company; they thought they would lose too much business if they ignored 50 percent. I responded by saying, "Let's not ignore that 50 percent. Let's turn those over to an inside sales team and focus our outbound energy on half of the accounts we are calling on face-to-face."

ASK THE SALES DOCTOR

NEW PERSON TO NEW TERRITORY

Debbie asks, "How do you start with a brand new idea in a brand new company to a brand new audience? I have a great opportunity I'm really excited about, yet it's outside my previous background and contacts. What are my chances for success?"

"One should never despair too soon."
—Frederick the Great

ANSWER

You're starting with a brand new idea in a brand new company to a brand new audience. I would call that the triple whammy.

You are what's called a trailblazer or a pioneer. The reason I call it "trailblazing" is to make people think about what happened to the great settlers as they charged across America from East to West. What happened to many of those trailblazers? Many of them never made it. That's the image you should have in mind when you have a new product and a new company you're trying to sell to new people. Prepare for the maximum amount of rejection. What I'm saying is up to 90 percent of the people you contact are going to say, "No thank you. Not interested. Once you get a track record call me back." You're going to hear every excuse you've ever imagined, and you're going to hear a lot of excuses you've never imagined.

Again, does this mean you're going to fail? The answer is no. First, you must absolutely believe in yourself. You have to have an unshakeable belief that even if ninety out of a hundred people say no, it's only because they don't know enough, or they don't know enough yet. It's not no, never they are saying—it's just not yet or maybe. Next, you have to be neutral as to the outcome of every approach you make. That means if you make ten approaches and the first ten people that day say no, you have to still be enthusiastic. On the eleventh call, you might just get someone to say, "Yes, I'll take a look at it."

You can only show the opportunity and ask people if they're interested. You cannot control the outcome. Take away all the energy about the negative responses and recognize that you are the person who can be neutral as to the outcome, and simply wait for the positive responses to come your way.

Here's another idea. Turn it into a game. Keep track of your statistics and see if you can beat the odds. What do I mean by that? If you're calling in your area with a new product, a new company, and a brand new audience, you're going to have to make—now check this out—a hundred contacts to get ten people who are interested. Again, that's that 90 percent rejection rate. If you reach those ten people who are interested, three will be so interested that you can take the next step—setting the appointment. Now they're in the sales funnel. And of those three, one of them will do business in a short amount of time.

If you need five people to sell this product or service to, be prepared to make five hundred contacts, which would take you several weeks. Keep your own stats. Maybe you can beat the odds. Maybe instead of ten out of a hundred interested, you could move that up to twenty. Well, you've just doubled your chance of success—if you contact twenty people, you're going to get six who are seriously interested, and two of them are going to become clients. That's how you keep score.

As always, we have to practice persistence. We have to remember what Winston Churchill said, "Never give up. Never, never, never, never, never."

This was an excellent way to attack the problem. In fact, the owner was so excited about the results that we ended up doing the same process twice more and at the end of the process the top fifteen salespeople each had between twenty-five and forty accounts.

This is why Total Selling includes a sales plan component. Why we do the things we do is often as important, or more important, than what we do and how we do it. This is why focusing on the plan is so important for salespeople.

Chapter Six

Creating Your Sales Plan

"As long as you're going to be thinking anyway, think big."—*Donald Trump*

Well readers, we've accomplished a lot to this point, and you're well on your way to becoming a Total Salesperson. I can hardly contain my excitement when I think about the ideas I'm about to share; they have helped me so much in my professional and personal life. You are embarking into a new dimension of understanding yourself, your goals, your dreams, your ambitions, and your sales success. It is your opportunity to combine the intellectual understanding of the concepts presented here with the level of desire that is in your heart and combine them into an undeniably powerful set of ideals. I hope you are excited too.

The Excitement about Sales Planning

One of the great aspects of having a good sales plan is that we can actually bring the future into the present, plan for it, and, therefore, predict the future. Read that sentence again. This should be one of the most exciting things you've ever read as a salesperson.

What I'm saying is that with a sound sales plan, we can actually attain virtually any goal we set for ourselves.

Earl Nightingale, a famous motivational speaker and radio personality from the 1950s through the 1970s, had a saying that I have written down and carried with me in my wallet for well over twenty years. "Success is the progressive realization of a predetermined, worthwhile ideal or goal."

What Earl Nightingale was saying, and what I very strongly believe in my heart, is that success—in terms of joy in our career, a certain financial status, the home we live in, the car we drive, the people with whom we socialize, the accounts we open, or however we define success—is progressive realization. "Progressive" means that it happens step-by-step, day-by-day, call-by-call, success-by-success, and failure-by-failure. "Realization" means that we can actually make it happen—we can realize it and we can recognize it.

"Predetermined" means that we can plan for it in advance. We can be futurists. We can be predeterminists. We can understand what the future is before we get there. How exciting is that?

Let's look at the "worthwhile" part of that quote. Again, worthwhile to whom? Worthwhile to us. Not worthwhile to your boss, your coach, your parent, your ancestors—important to you.

And then finally, the ideal or goal. That's the end point. What is it to which we're aspiring? The ideal, the goal, is the top of the mountain. What we're saying here is that the essence of sales planning is being aware of being able to bring the future into the present and plan for it. I'm excited just thinking about that.

Well Begun is Half Done

Many salespeople do not turn their goals into reality because they tend to confuse activity with productivity. Most salespeople want to feel as if they are making a contribution to their company and their own careers. And so instead of focusing on doing the right things, we focus on just being busy.

This is one of the great tragedies of being a failure in sales. Having a sound sales plan is one of the most important decisions a salesperson can ever make to avoid failure.

As the Greek philosopher, Aristotle advised 2,300 years ago, "Well begun is half done." This axiom is telling us that if we have a sound plan and we move in a direction of our goals or plans, this good beginning will help us attain our goals.

We can make great decisions for ourselves in terms of what we're going to say on the phone, who we're going to call, what our values are in the marketplace, where the best fit is with our potential customer base, and many other factors that we actually can control. It's all a matter of doing the planning up front so that once we start acting on our plan, we are leading ourselves toward success and away from failure.

ASK THE SALES DOCTOR

WHEN NEW TO UNDER-PERFORMING TERRITORY

Tom asks, "I'm brand new to selling and have taken over a territory that has been under-served for over a year. The customers will deliver about half my quota based on being neglected. How can I get going quickly and earn the business of my customers and grow my territory 50 percent in one year?"

ANSWER

You're actually in a pretty good position. It's unfortunate that your territory has been under-served, but you do have customers. So that's the first place to start. Imagine, Tom, if you were in the type of business where you had nothing going and no clients, and you were starting in a brand new "cold" territory. You'd really have to scramble to create 100 percent of your quota.

In this case you've already got some business. You want to go back to all the current clients who are currently buying from your company. And if it's a face-to-face business you're in, get on the phone. Make the call. Tell them you want to see them on a particular date, and book yourself into an appointment. In other words, work by appointment. Just don't show up, or tell them you're going to stop by when you're in the area. It demeans them, and it demeans you. So you call the clients up. Get a firm appointment.

And once you're there, warm up. Don't go into business right away unless you're involved with those one or two percent that don't want to talk about anything but business. And they'll let you know. The rest will want to talk about what's new with you, what's new with them. Some safe things to talk about are the weather, or the local sports team. I'd stay away from politics or religion or whatever's on the front page of the newspaper. Or just talk in general about how's business going, some industry specific things. Just warm up the conversation.

And now before you do anything that involves offering a product or service, ask them what problems they've had that you could take care of. A lot of customers aren't going to get into a buying mode unless they have dealt with problems that have been troubling them. Either an order was shipped in improperly, or there was a shortage, or something was broken, or something didn't go right or there was a special order that is lost in the system somewhere...Your main goal is to get the person open to new ideas, and the best way to do that is to take care of problems.

Then ask what's new with them. Maybe there's something new in their business, an emerging trend. Maybe there's a new product that they're getting a lot of interest in, or a new service that they've been asked to provide. Just get them talking about their business. And then talk about what their current needs might be. If they've bought a particular type of product...Your question doesn't say what business you're in. But let's say you're in the nurseryman's supply business, you might start asking them what some of their current needs are, fertilizer, perennials, annuals, seeds, whatever.

Once you identify what their current needs are and take care of those, then you move on to offering a new idea or a new product or a new service. The easiest way to grow your business is to keep offering new ideas and new services to your current client base. And a lot of the times you say, "Oh, they probably read the brochures. They understand our marketing guidelines. They know what we offer." And you know what? The sad truth is they only know what they buy from you today. So your job is to expand the horizons.

And then – here is the absolute, jet-fueled technique – ask permission to ask them for referrals. Tell them that you're new to the territory, and that you obviously want to grow, and you're actually trying to grow your business by 50 percent, and you want to do that by maintaining your service level. Ask them if you know anybody you could be calling on, because referrals are five times more likely to buy than people who don't come to you from a strong referral.

Here's another great idea. You've got lots of inactive clients, or orphan accounts as I call them because your territory was under-served by the person that was there before you. Go into those files, give those people a call. And then just tell them, "Look, you've been orphaned by my company, and I'm calling to adopt you." And it's such a cute line. The people will laugh; they'll like it. And they'll probably give you the appointment to come see them.

You should also get involved in something—Rotary or a Lion's or a Kiwanis or a Chamber of Commerce or Optimists organizations. I'm not talking about a trade organization that serves the needs of your business, because you're going to meet people just like you. What I mean is, expand your horizons and become involved in organizations that are outside of your core trade areas.

So, Tom, you asked a great eyedropper question, and I gave you the fire hose answer. But I've got a very soft spot in my heart for new salespeople. In fact, one of the reasons I started my business is because I hated seeing about one-third of salespeople new to the business fail every year. I knew I could change that because the turnover in the companies where I worked when I was a sales manager was always under 10 percent.

Every Building Begins with a Strong Foundation

If we're in the building trade and we're building a house for one of our customers, wouldn't we have to understand the fundamentals, the building blocks, the principals of home building? Of course we would.

Like building a strong house, sales success begins with having an effective sales plan. It is the foundation built on level ground. It is the structure on which the balance of our sales activities rest.

If we built our sales plan the way contractors build buildings, the way doctors plan a surgery, the way architects plan skyscrapers, we would ensure that we would be successful in sales.

Discovering our Core Competencies

It's important for us to focus on our strengths. This does not mean that we ignore our weaknesses, that we hide our heads in the sand about the areas in which we're not as strong. We have to know why people want to do business with us and really focus on what we are good at.

You're a pitcher with an average curve ball and change-up, but an unbelievably fabulous fast ball; when the game was on the line and you knew you only had one pitch

> **"A man's fortune has its form given to it by his habits."—*Anonymous***

that you could use to strike out the batter with two people on base and two outs, in the bottom of the ninth inning, what pitch would you throw? Obviously you'd throw your fast ball. Like the baseball pitcher trying to get the other side out, salespeople really need to focus on their strikeout pitch.

You can't be all things to all people. You can't be the low cost provider, the superior service provider, and the most efficient operations company. How do we make sure we convey what we do well to our customers? How do we "accentuate the positive?"

You're Not "Too" Anything

> **"Nothing in life just happens. You have to have the stamina to meet the obstacles and overcome them."**
> **—*Golda Meir***

I once worked with a salesperson who was not sure that she would be successful in sales because she was too young.

I asked her, "How long has your company been in business?" She responded that they had been in business for over fifty years. Then I asked, "The other people that work in your company, how long have they been doing what they do?" She told me that the company was very well-respected in its industry and had a great track record.

Next, I asked her why she thought that they had hired her. I also followed up by asking her what the customers would think once they knew about the company's experience and her youthfulness. I asked her if she thought it would be a drawback in her business and she responded that she was not sure.

The point is, you're never "too" anything to be successful in sales. You're never too old, too young, too poor, too uneducated, too educated, too jaded, too jaundiced, too innocent, and too ignorant—anything that we're talking about in the Total Selling model and anything that you're reading in this book can be learned and applied by all of us. You're never "too" anything to start being successful. You're never "too" anything to organize a successful sales plan.

Business Planning for the Total Salesperson

If you've ever had the opportunity to be involved in management or run a business of your own, you know that business planning is a nonnegotiable part of business. Yet, how many salespeople do you know who actually possess a written business plan that covers:

- their goals for the year
- where that business is going to come from
- contingency plans for when things don't go exactly the way they are planned
- a budget for accomplishing the various tasks that are set out
- a time frame with milestones, deadlines, and responsibilities

What I've just described is the essence of business planning for salespeople. A sales plan is simply a business plan focused on top-line performance that makes sure all the actions taken on a daily basis are part of the overall plan.

Doing the Right Things Versus Doing Things Right

Sales planning is equivalent to being a sales leader. In the world of business, leaders are the people who establish the goals on which an organization is going to focus. It's called "doing the right things." Now, management in large organizations is a slightly different function and that is called "doing things right." Sales planning in the Total Selling model is all about doing the right things. Later, when we talk about sales practice (which is in essence self-management for salespeople), we'll talk about doing things right.

ASK THE SALES DOCTOR

QUESTION
Theresa asks, "Are you sure that sales planning really works?"

"Goals are dreams with deadlines."
—Diana Scharf Hunt

ANSWER
Yes, and I'll tell you why from a personal standpoint. There was a year when I decided I was going to work pretty much without goals. That I had actually worked very hard for three years and attained much of what I sought to accomplish, and I thought, well, I'll just see what happens this year. I won't really set any standards for myself. That year I had nothing written down, I had no sales plan as far as how I was going to accomplish my goals, and I had a very average year.

> I find that there is an amazing amount of energy and strength and power behind having your sales plan written out and in front of you all the time. It helps you focus on what you need to do. It helps you focus on why you are doing the things you do and helps you to overcome the inertia of just letting things happen. I can't emphasize enough the importance of sales planning

Setting Sales Goals

> "What is important is not that there are uncontrollable events in our lives, but how we respond to them."
> —*Hyrum W. Smith*

Setting sales goals sounds simple, yet in practice can be quite complicated. In my view salespeople start with a list of goals that is massive in scope—it's more like a wish list than a goals list. One of the keys to understanding how to be a successful goal-setter is to refine or focus that list. I'm a big fan of simplifying things, and one of the gifts that I have been given is the ability to take rather complex subjects and make them simple.

This is the same thing we want to do in goal-setting. You have to really understand what it is we are trying to accomplish and make it so simple that we could explain it to our third grader.

The Myth of "No" Goals

I've read a lot of books that talk about how goal-setting is really passé. These books and articles discuss living without goals, going with the flow, being in the moment. Now I'm a big believer that we really need to enjoy who we are and what we do. We cannot afford to rue or feel remorseful about the past, nor can we have anxiety about the future—these are losing strategies.

"What's important is that one strives to achieve a goal."
—Ronald Reagan

It is very important to be *in the moment*. Yet, while we are in the moment we have to know where we've come from and where we're going, and that's why goals are so important.

Imagine if an airplane trying to get from New York to Los Angeles had no goals. Now wouldn't that be ridiculous? It would zig-zag across the country, run out of fuel, and put all the passengers at risk. Airplanes have goals. The goal is to get from New York to Los Angeles in a particular amount of time.

Heck, even squirrels have goals. Squirrels have a goal of finding and eating lots of nuts in the fall and burying a whole bunch more so that once the trees stop producing nuts, they have a way to survive the winter. A goal-less squirrel would die in the dead of winter.

For most people, focusing on just a few goals works best. We have to really ask ourselves, "Why are we doing the things we are doing?" "Why are we trying to accomplish certain things?" "What is our personal mission?" We really have to focus on the why, the purpose behind the goal.

After that we need to break the goal down into small, doable action points. I've worked with many salespeople over the years who have big goals. But when it comes time to put together the action plan, they are stuck because they don't know where to start.

Imagine if I just decided one day to write this book and say, "I'm going to write the book *Total Selling*. I'm going to sit down at my desk and think about all the ideas—and tomorrow the book will be done." That's outrageous and impossible.

I must have a specific plan of how I'm going to accomplish writing the book and schedule the appropriate amount of time every day to take the action. That's where a book concept begins, where an outline is established, where the time is set aside to sit in front of the computer and write. These are all the action plans, and too many times in sales we fail because we're not allocating the appropriate amount of time to building our business.

The next step is to take action. Once we have a sales plan or a goal in mind, and when we put together the action plan to make it happen, the most important task is to take action. Make it happen. This is why the Nike slogan "Just Do It" resonates with so many millions of people all over the world. When push comes to shove, there's a time to plan and there's a time to act. That's why the expression "Ready-Aim-Fire" has the "Fire" component. That's why in a running race the person who is in charge of the starting gun says "On your mark, get set, go!" They don't say "On your mark, get set, stay there." They don't say "On the mark, get set, keep set, keep setting."

No, in order to run in the race, to win the race, you have to "go" and that is really one of the most important aspects of being successful with a sales plan.

A Snapshot of Your Business

"Unless we change our direction, we are likely to end up where we are headed."—*Old Chinese Proverb*

Let's get very specific about what a sales plan means for salespeople. The first question we need to ask ourselves is this: Where do we want to end up?

For most salespeople, this means an annual sales goal. This could be a quota delivered to you by someone in your organization. This is the weakest type of goal because it's something we haven't bought into as individuals. It's just an idea that someone has given us.

I've had many discussions with sales managers and vice presidents of sales and they talk about how they're going to divide their overall corporate goal by area, by division, by region, by sector, by salesperson, and everyone will be assigned their quota. My response has always been, "Well, how do you know that the salesperson who is way down the line at the bottom of that planning exercise isn't satisfied with half of the amount of sales that you are expecting at corporate? What if that person has been working really hard for five years and has come to a plateau? Maybe you're looking for another 10–15 percent increase out of that person and they're ready to kick back and rest on their laurels."

There's a disconnect between the individual goal and the corporate goal. It's a very interesting question that we need to ask ourselves: "Where are we going to end up?" We have to align the corporate goals with the individual goals.

Where are we today? If I decided that I wanted to take a train to Seattle, Washington, I would then have to ask myself, "Where am I today? Am I in Chicago, Miami, or Spokane?" In other words, we have to know where we are today so we know how far we are away from the goal.

One of the aspects of knowing where we are is to conduct a current client analysis so that we know who our clients are and how much business we've received from them over the last five years. Is the trend going up or going down? Is there something that's happening in our customer's business that is either increasing or decreasing the amount of business we're getting?

We have to know where we are today by asking questions such as these:

- What does the economy look like?
- What's our particular environment based on our geographic area?
- Are companies moving in or moving out of our area?

- What is the housing market doing?
- What are large corporations in our geographic area doing?
- Who are emerging competitors?
- Are there some entrenched competitors in our marketplace?

These are all questions we have to answer to know where we are today. If we don't have a good handle on where we are today and what the relative marketplace is, how are we ever going to put together the plan to reach our goals? It will never happen unless we not only know where we want to end up, but where we are today.

ASK THE SALES DOCTOR

NEVER BAD MOUTH COMPETITION

Robin asks, "I'm facing a serious competitive threat for the first time in my territory after being dominant for over ten years.

"Each year, one bad habit rooted out, in time ought to make the worst man good."
—Benjamin Franklin

My new competitor is very aggressive, bad-mouths my company, and generally is becoming a real pain. What can I do to fight back?"

ANSWER

You've been the dominant player for over ten years, Robin. And my question is—I'm not trying to insult you—have you rested on your laurels? Have you gotten lazy about your clients? I'm not accusing you of that. I'm just asking you to consider that possibility. Because if you have, one of the solutions is to remember what it was like when you were not the dominant player in that territory and start getting back into that hustle where you are out hustling this competitor, and you have that energy and enthusiasm to go back after that particular business that is being attacked by this competitor. So that's my first reaction.

I've got a really strong point to make. You mentioned that this competitor is bad-mouthing your company. Let me caution you. No matter what you do, don't get down in the mud and slug it out with this other competitor. Don't go on the Internet and try and dig up dirt on them so that when they bad-mouth you, you can bad-mouth them better. That is a losing proposition. If you're hearing from your clients that this particular competitor said such-and-such about you, or they're telling your customers how wonderful they are, all you need to do is say, "Hey, you know what? They're a great company." Then pause (one-one-thousand, two-one-thousand) and go right back into your own attributes or your own benefits.

Don't get into those battles where you're trying to slam them and they're trying to slam you. It's a no-win proposition, and it makes you look bad in front of your customer base because they think, "Well, gee whiz, why all of a sudden do you have to be slamming your competitors? I've been loyal to you, Robin, for ten years. Just treat me the way I've been treated, and you will get that business, or at least you'll have the right to earn that business, and continue to have that relationship."

How Will We Get There?

We also have to find out how we're going to get to where we're going. There are only three ways to grow a business. You can either retain the business you

> "The great end of life is not knowledge but action."
> —*Thomas Henry Huxley*

have, grow the business you have, or go out and find brand new business.

We have to ask ourselves what percent of our time we're going to allocate for each of those three activities. For instance, if we have a very strong customer base and we know that customer base is going to grow significantly within our planning period, it's going to be very difficult for us to go out there and find new business. Sometimes new business can take a year or more to bring to closure, and if we are very busy servicing and growing our current accounts, we are not going to be able to reach our goals by developing new business.

We have to know where we're going and how we're going to get there.

Our Strengths, Weaknesses, Opportunities, and Threats

One of the ways to find out exactly where we are in terms of the strength and power of our business is to examine who we are, what we do, what we're good at, and where we're weak. A classic business approach is to use what's called a SWOT analysis, which stands for Strengths-Weaknesses-Opportunities-Threats. For salespeople I suggest a slight variation on a SWOT analysis. We ought to do several SWOT analyses:

1. Focus on our company
2. Focus on us as individuals
3. Focus on our key competitors

On the top left side write the word "strength" on the top right write the word "weakness" in the middle of the page on the left side write the word "opportunity" in middle of the page on the right side write the word "threat."

Strength	Weakness
Opportunities	Threats

Begin by looking analyzing yourself and your business on the left side of the page. First, write down all the different areas in which you as an individual and your company are strong. This would be a great place to list where your strengths lie in terms of product, service, offering, warranties, guarantees, image, delivery, terms, and special services provided. Really get creative and write down all the possible features of your company (what your company does or what the feature is) or the benefit (why it's important to the people who buy it).

Don't sell yourself short in this exercise. Keep writing until you come up with all kinds of strengths that your company brings to the marketplace.

In the same vein, on the middle part of the left side of the page, where you've written "opportunities," think in creative terms and outside the box. In terms of opportunities for your company, think about your current customers, add-on sales to current customers, referred prospects, targeted prospects, new business opportunities, completely outrageous ways that your products and services might fit with new businesses or outrageous business products that would fit in with your current customer base. Be absolutely noncensoring and let your imagination run wild.

Now when it comes to the right side of the page on the top right where you've written "weakness," be realistic, but don't beat yourself up about it. The reason I mention this is that in many seminars where I ask people to do a SWOT analysis, they write down three or four items on the left side of the page (strengths and opportunities) then spend about twenty years writing down all the things on the right side of the page. We diminish our strengths, and we can't wait to talk about our weakness, which conversely are usually the strengths of the competition.

What I want to do is break that mold—focus your energy on the left side of your page and just be realistic on the right side. So indeed write down weaknesses that you have in the marketplace, the weaknesses that your company has in a competitive situation, and generate a reasonable list.

Then in the middle on the right, list threats to your company. These could be environmental threats or overall macroeconomic trends that are a threat to your business. Again, be realistic, but don't go hog wild.

Competitors' Strengths, Weaknesses, Opportunities, and Threats

Now it's time to do a 180-degree view SWOT analysis on our competitors. In this exercise we focus on the right side of the page and write down all the weaknesses and all the threats that we or the environment could provide to our competition. On the left side of the page, be realistic, but don't go overboard. Just list some serious strengths and opportunities that your competition might have.

I suggest that you do this exercise for maybe one, two, or three of your major competitors. First, doing this exercise enables us to understand that we really bring a lot of value to the marketplace and it builds our confidence level. Second, it helps us feel stronger about how we match up against our competition because we see that they're not some big hairy monster that can crush us with a step, but rather a reasonable competitor who we match up against pretty well.

SALES IDEA

THROW YOUR STRIKE-OUT PITCH
"Be like a postage stamp—stick to one thing until you get there."
—Josh Billings

Knowing what your strike-out pitch is—doing those things that really play to your strengths—is a great idea. Another way of looking at that is to say "accentuate the positive." Here's an idea presented earlier, with a twist.

Take out a clean sheet of paper and write down all of your strengths. Write down every single thing that you bring to the table: all the great benefits, all the great features, all the great guarantees and warranties that you provide your customer base. Write them down in terms of what it means to your customers. That's part one.

Here's the twist. Part two is to ask your best three to five clients to do the very same thing. Send them an email or a letter, call them on the phone, or take them out to lunch and say, "I'm looking at the reasons why people do business with me. Can you write down all the strengths of my company and our relationship and what it means to you based on what you know about my company?"

And you know what? You will be shocked at the great feedback you get from your customers. They're going to come up with many ideas that you hadn't even thought of. That's part two.

So, in part one you write down all your strengths. In part two have one of your best customers do the same thing. And the final part of this sales idea is to find the highest-leveraged, most wonderful item that shows up on both lists and use that as your strike-out pitch. When you call new people, let them know that's what you and your customers think you provide best.

> Lead with your fastball. Lead with your best pitch. Accentuate your most positive.
>
> **Action: Write down the three to five people you would ask to do this.**

Creating Your Value Proposition

Someone once said, "A man who doesn't stand for something will fall for anything." When I think about value propositions, this is the quote that pops into my head. The question ought to be, "What do we stand for?" What do we really feel is the biggest attribute or reason for being in business that we want to represent in the marketplace?

In my business, for example, I stand for customized sales education that is non-manipulative, professional, easy to apply, and based on common sense. When people ask me if I can do customer service programs, I know that I could, but I don't. If people ask me if I can put together a list of the 15 most effective closes and teach them to their salespeople, I know that I could, but I don't. If people ask me if I can come up some new outrageously unique way of teaching salespeople how to be actors, I probably could, but I don't.

What I'm getting at is I know exactly what it is that I stand for, and once you know what you stand for it really helps you be successful in sales. There are generally three different types of approaches that most businesses take in the marketplace.

One of the main attributes that companies can stand for is for operational efficiency. Operational efficiency means that your company can get items, merchandise, products or services from point A to point B more efficiently than your competition. Many companies come to mind as examples of this, but Wal-Mart is probably the best.

Another attribute that some people stand for is exemplary customer service. This means that your customers know that whatever happens, whatever the situation, the customer comes first.

A company that exemplifies this attribute is Nordstrom. They go the extra mile for every customer. There are many stories that are told about Nordstrom, such as the one story about the wardrobe consultant who drove through a snowstorm to deliver the tuxedo shirt that was left at the store, to make sure the groom wasn't standing at the end of the aisle bare-chested on his wedding day.

Another attribute some companies stand for is technological superiority. They stand for innovation and technology, for being on the leading edge (and sometimes the bleeding edge). They take the creative "point" in their marketplace. A company that comes to mind is the early Microsoft - they stood for bringing the best technology to everyone's desktop.

So you get the idea that there are various aspects within any business in which you can lay out your value proposition. The way to think about that is to ask yourself, "What do I stand for?"

Current Situation

Again, moving along with the theme of understanding where we are today in our business, it's important for us to understand our current situation. In many businesses for which I've consulted, my customers really didn't know where they stood with their customers, the outlook for the upcoming year; or whether they would garner the same amount of business they enjoyed the previous year, a portion of that business, or have to rebuild their business.

Any analysis of where you want to lead your business begins with a discussion of the current situation. The best way to do this is to go through your account list and stratify the accounts from best to worst, from highest revenue to lowest revue, from greatest amount of profit to least amount of profit.

In this way you can see that, if you're like most businesses, the 80/20 rule will apply. This means that about 80 percent of your revenue will be generated by 20 percent of your customers. It also means that 80 percent of your problems, concerns, or price battles are going to come from 20 percent of your clients as well. Look at your best customers, that top 20 percent that generate 80 percent of the revenue, and decide if you're going to be able to generate that same type of business in the coming planning period, or if you're at risk anywhere.

Before we can predict where we're going to end up, we have to know where we are. An analysis of the current situation and our current customers is a great place to start.

Business Gap Analysis

"I always wanted to be somebody, but I should have been more specific."—*Lily Tomlin*

The Business Gap Analysis is a strategic planning tool that enables sales professionals to evaluate where they are today and compare it to their sales goals so they can take action for maximum results.

Example: Salesperson Smith would like to know how to grow his business for 2004, based on his current 2003 business and experience with his past clients. His business looks like this:

a. 2003 actual sales: $1 million

b. Five year average percent old business lost per year:
   10 percent ($100,000)

c. If nothing changes, 2004 sales projection $900,000

d. Desired business 2004 sales increase
   15 percent ($1.15 million)

e. Gap =$1.15 million - $900,000 = $250,000

f. Five year average current client growth
   10 percent ($90,000)

g. Gap with current client factored in = $160,000

h. Average sale per new account $10,000
i. New accounts needed to cover the gap   16

Now Salesperson Smith knows exactly what to do in order to meet his 2004 goals - he needs to develop16 new clients, and he needs to grow his current accounts by 10 percent.

Amount of New Business Needed

Once we have completed our Gap Analysis, we know exactly how much new business we need. Most people underestimate the effort it takes to bring new business in the door. New-business development skills are the most desirable within any organization; they are the skills that the fewest salespeople actually possess. Most new-business development activities lead to the maximum amount of rejection because such efforts mean calling on people who are not familiar with the company and what it stands for, and calling on people who already have pre-existing relationships with our competition.

So unless something is broken—that is to say, the potential customer we're calling on is very unhappy with their current provider or vendor—we face an uphill battle to win that business over to our side. As a rule of thumb, if we were starting with a list of nonreferred prospects, we would need about a hundred companies with whom we don't have any relationship in order to develop a list of ten companies that might have an interest in working with us at some time in the future.

So what we've determined here is that approximately 10 percent of the doors we attempt to open will actually be opened to us. In my experience, using that information as a springboard, we are in the position of leveraging what I call the 10-3-1 rule. This means that of 10 people who have some type of interest in working with us, roughly 3 of those people will agree to talk to us in a meaningful way about their needs and the way our services match up with their needs, and 1 of those 3 will end up doing business with us within that sales cycle.

So what we see is that 10 qualified prospects lead to 3 opportunities, and that leads to 1 piece of new business gained. This is something important for all of us to know, and it's one of the key sales metrics of which any salesperson needs to be aware.

> "Every great and commanding movement in the annals of the world is the triumph of enthusiasm."
>
> —*Ralph Waldo Emerson*

The Elevator Speech

When we meet someone for the first time, we like to get to know who they are and what they do. Eventually the conversation will come around to you. They're going to ask you who you are and what you do. This is your opportunity to create a unique positioning statement.

A lot of people go about this the wrong way. They start talking about their title, or they start defining themselves by their topic or what they do or their position in the company. That's all a bunch of nonsense. The best way to position yourself is to think about what you would say to someone if you had a chance to be with him in an elevator. It's what I call your elevator speech. From the time the doors close until the time you get off at your floor, how much time do you usually have? Well, it's not that much. It's ten, fifteen, maybe twenty seconds.

What we're looking for is some simple statement that's easy to tell, that would be easy for them to tell somebody else about if they heard it. It's not based on title or subject matter. It's something that provokes a "how do you do that?" response.

Let me give you an example. If someone asks me, "What do you do?" I say, "I work with salespeople who want to maintain and grow their businesses, and I work with sales executives who want to help their salespeople be their best." What I've defined is something that's very easy. It's repeatable. If somebody says, "What does that Warren guy do?" they say, "Oh, he's the guy that works with salespeople to help them grow and maintain their business, and he works with sales executives to help their salespeople to become better at what they do."

Notice how it's really simple eighth grade language, and it's something that someone can take and repeat to someone else. Every time I say that, the response is, "Well, how do you do that?" And that's exactly what I want them to say. I follow up by saying, "Based on technology, tools and techniques that I have created, I lead seminars, I advise people, and I have a line-up of educational materials that I can share with people as well."

So now they know that as far as what my benefits are, I can help by advising people, by speaking, and by offering educational materials that are there even when I'm not.

Part Three
Sales Practice

Chapter Seven

Self-Management for Sales Professionals

"The ability to concentrate and to use your time well is everything."—*Lee Iacocca*

As evidenced throughout *Total Selling*, I am a very strong believer in taking action. You may remember the earlier where we talked about the slogans that end in action: ready, set, go!; ready, aim, fire! Sales practice is all about taking action and measuring progress toward our goals. If we think about a sales plan as the big picture, then sales practice becomes the little picture. This is not to say that it's diminished in terms of importance. To the contrary, I've run into many sales people who had excellent sales skills—that is to say, they understood sales process and had great ambitions and concrete ideas on how they were going to launch and maintain a successful sales career.

In most cases, the areas where salespeople have the least amount of skill or run into the most problems is in the area of using high quality sales practices. Let me give you an example. I was working with a young salesperson on the East Coast several years back who, for a number of reasons, had to put up big numbers. It was important to him, important to his company, and important to his family. After interviewing him for several hours, I realized that the potentially fatal flaw in what he was doing was that he really could not control his day-to-day activities. He was scattered. He was like the absent-minded professor in that his behaviors were always just a little bit "off." He was a day late and a dollar short. If the decision was made on a Tuesday, he'd call on a Wednesday. He just didn't have the vision of what effective sales practices were. I spent many hours with him explaining what you're about to read—and the good news is that he was able to use the ideas effectively and become very successful in his sales career. I can't emphasize this point enough. Taking action is absolutely one of the most important topics for the professional salesperson.

But don't think you are off the hook if you are now a relatively new salesperson like the young man in the above example. If you are already an experienced salesperson classified as an underperformer, underachiever, or overachiever (see page 26 in Chapter One), you will find that you can squeeze more and more minutes and hours out of the day by utilizing effective sales practices. Self-management for sales professionals is a benefit to all salespeople—whether new, old, experienced, inexperienced, struggling, or at the top of their game. Let's get started.

Once we have a clearly defined sales plan, effective sales practice becomes our road map. Sales practice is what we utilize in order to accomplish our sales plan. It is our monitoring and feedback system. It allows is to keep track of our time and control the events in our lives. Another way of looking at this is to say that detailing our plan through our sales practices enables us to do the right thing at the right time.

> **"Say no to unimportant things that pull you away from more important ones."—*Success Tip***

It's important to understand the concept of *non-discretionary time*. Commitments, to others, and ourselves are times in our lives where we know we're going to be scheduled for a certain amount of time and during that time, we won't be able to work on anything else. The point is this: Scheduled activities drive out unscheduled activities (a point we will return to later). So imagine that you wanted to set one new appointment and you knew that one hour of uninterrupted outbound calling would yield one appointment. It sounds simple. It's simple yet not easy.

I've observed hundreds of salespeople who know that they need to carve out one hour of time, yet never do it. The only way to succeed is to make an appointment with yourself for that one hour, say from 3:00 to 4:00 PM and close your door. Now if somebody said to you, "Hey can you get together between 3:00 and 4:00 PM, go to the conference room, and talk about a plan for Crocker Industries?" You would say "No, I'm sorry. I have a previous commitment." This example demonstrates the power of creating non-discretionary time. We can bring an incredible amount of control into our daily sales practices by making a commitment to scheduling the activities that are part of our sales plan. This is just one example of how to create a winning sales practice—you will learn many more in this chapter on self-management.

The Five Elements of Effective Sales Practice

There are five basic elements of a good sales practice. The first element is to *create a list* of our selling activities. Breaking down our plan into activities enhances the road map by which we'll reach our destination. It shows us what needs to be done, how far away we are from the attainment of the goal, what resources we'll need, what commitment we'll need to make, and how much energy we'll need to guarantee success. Many people find that either their goal needs to be adjusted because of a lack of time to commit to a goal, or other commitments need to be changed so that a goal can be achieved, once they see how long the list of activities can become.

The second element is to make sure that each activity is *small* enough, based on how much time and resources we are able to commit to the goal. Many people create lists that really are additional goals masquerading as a list of activities. This makes people procrastinate, or worse yet, give up, because they feel that the task at hand is too large. When I wrote my first book, *The Six Steps to Excellence in Selling*, I found that understanding how small to make my individual activities on my list was a major success factor in moving from idea to publication in six months.

The third element is to *prioritize* our list of activities. People who do not prioritize experience what I call the "whiplash effect" because what happens to them is that they start looking from the top of the list to the bottom of the list, trying to find something they can do quickly or something that's very easy to do. The head snapping to and fro as it moves up and down the list causes the "whiplash."

You can prevent whiplash by sorting your activities by priority. There are activities that are more important to us than others and we need a system of ranking so we know what we ought to be working on first, second, third, and so on. The way we first prioritize our activities is by using alphabetical letters. The first and most vital activities on our list we call *A* priorities. *A* means the activity is vital, critical, and urgent to our success. The *B* activities would be those things that we consider important, but not as vital, critical, or urgent to our success—not necessarily as important as our vital activities, but nonetheless, important to us. *C* activities would stand for activities that are somewhat important to us. We would probably achieve our goal without them, and they would either be icing on the cake, or would make our achievement be that much better if they were accomplished.

When we've completed prioritizing our activities into *A*, *B* and *C*, we will most probably find that we have more than one *A*, *B*, and *C*. Next, you can apply the Theory of 1-2-3 by going through your list again and prioritizing the *As*, *Bs*, and *Cs*, starting with the *As*, in terms of how vital, critical, or urgent to your success they are. You will then have a list that reads: *A1*, *A2*, *A3*, *B1*, *B2*, *B3*, and so on.

The fourth element is *setting deadlines* to actually begin. Many people set deadlines to complete a task or activity yet very few people schedule deadlines to begin a task. "Well begun is half done," goes the saying. It's true. Set deadlines to begin activities. You'll find that the act of deciding to begin will give you a lot of momentum.

"Learn this balance: less procrastinating equals less stress."—Success Tip

---

Closely related to deadlines is the fifth element, which is *tracking your progress*. How many times do we have a to-do list that we're working on, and we get to the point where we've completed an item and we get to put a check mark next to it, or an X, or draw a line through it. Doesn't that feel great? We can say to ourselves, Yes, I've finished that and now I'm going to draw a line through it, or mark it off, or put a big check mark next to it. It's the small step along the journey and shows us in a concrete manner that we're making progress toward our goal.

SALES IDEA

GETTING UNSTUCK

"Try? There is no try. There is only do or not do."
—Yoda, in The Empire Strikes Back

Have you ever found yourself in the position of not knowing what to do in pursuing business with a new prospect or growing your business with a current client? How about not being able to work through a tough obstacle or form of resistance? If you answered "yes" to either of the above questions, you're not alone. You're just plain stuck. Here's how you get unstuck. First, review the recent history of the particular account up to the present moment. Second, write down all the reasons why you might be stuck. Third, brainstorm potential options that would help you to get unstuck. Don't allow doubt to creep in. Accept all options that come to your mind no matter how crazy they seem.

Action: Contact the person on the phone, knowing that you have identified where you are stuck and that you possess many ways to get unstuck and move the sales process forward.

Effective Self-Management

"If you fail to control the events in your life, the events in your life will control you."—*Unknown*

Effective self-management is doing things right. This is distinguished from being effective at sales planning, which is doing the right things. There is a major difference between being busy doing things and being busy doing the right things. Got that?

Effective self-management means that we bring our energy and attention to those activities and events in our sales career that will help us reach our sales plan. That's why the essence of effective sales management is doing things in the most effective, efficient, and appropriate manner. There are a number of different issues we need to consider when talking about being effective self-managers.

SALES IDEA

THE FOUR DS

The best way to make changes in our use of time is to understand the "Four Ds of Self-Management."

DO what is vital. These are the activities that help us maintain and grow our business and are best done by us. Examples are meeting with a client to work on the relationship or introduce a new idea, making outbound calls to potential new clients, preparing for presentations, or working with centers of influence to expand our contacts.

DELEGATE the details. These are activities that can be done by others and managed by you to make sure that the actions have been completed. Examples are routine policy changes or notices, completing paperwork, filing, invoicing, requesting and sending out information, and routine correspondence.

DELAY what can wait. (This does not mean being late on commitments that we have previously made.) Examples are reading industry information, non-urgent, non-important phone calls, and paperwork that is not time sensitive.

DROP the time wasters. Examples are junk mail, junk email, people who aren't motivated to work and are looking

for other people to "hang out with", and interruptions that
re not urgent and not important.

Action: Look at your current to-do list. Write the appropriate method (do, delegate, delay, drop) by each task and actually do it that way today.

Managing Alphabetical and Chronological Information

There are two main types of information that we need to manage as sales professionals: alphabetical information and chronological information. Alphabetical information is any type of data or knowledge organized by the letters of the alphabet. Customer lists, prospect lists, catalogs, brochures, information sheets, and other such information all need to be stored alphabetically.

Most people have two alphabetical systems—one for their electronically stored information and one for their more traditional paper-stored information. I strongly recommend developing a system of file folders. The best way to do this is to get twenty-six file folders, put the letters A through Z on each folder, and store individual files accordingly.

This sounds like a simplistic idea, yet I have worked with many salespeople who didn't have a clue about how to organize this. I worked with one particular salesperson many years ago who had a mound of paper in the center of his desk. He asked me to come help him organize all the information. I told him to get twenty-six hanging file folders, twenty-six plastic tabs, twenty-six pieces of cardboard on which to write the letters of the alphabet, and two boxes of one-hundred-each manila third-cut file folders.

We painstakingly went through every piece of paper and categorized it. When we finally got to the bottom of the mound (five hours later), we located the most important piece of paper. This paper contained information on his best prospect and had been missing for about three months. You can readily see from this example the benefit of organizing your alphabetical information appropriately.

Closely related to these alphabetical files is a system that manages our chronological information. Chronological information is obviously driven by the clock and the calendar. It's so important for us to understand this concept, especially when it comes to reserving time for ourselves to do the appropriate activities to move ourselves forward in sales.

How many times have you come into your office and looked at your calendar and seen a blank space, meaning you had nothing scheduled? You probably said to yourself, "Oh, I'm going to be so productive today and accomplish so much." In reality, what happened? If you're like most people, you basically accomplished nothing and wasted a large part of the day.

Contrast this with the saying, "If you want something done properly, give it to a busy person," and you'll see that there's a tremendous benefit to learning how to manage your days through the use of chronological data. I suggest that you look at your goals and compare what you know is important to you with what you're actually doing during any given day. Then you ought to select various action items from your master goals list and schedule them into your day.

This is why understanding how our rhythms operate and how much time we actually have to do things are important lessons to learn. We need to manage by the hour, by the day, by the week, by the month, by the quarter, and by the year. It's so important for us to schedule time at the appropriate part of the day in order to set appointments, make outbound dials, do research, and write proposals. Every item that we should work on ought to be committed to writing in a chronological system.

You may ask, "Should I use paper or something electronic?" In my day-to-day sales management and sales education practice, I am constantly asked by people whether they should use a paper system, a computerized system, or a Web-based system (in which all the information resides on a server). My response has been the same for years, before the Web and even before computer-based systems: figure out what your needs are and then choose one system and utilize it exclusively. I can't emphasize this strongly enough. What this means is that if you decide you're going to use a paper system (Franklin Planner, Day Runner, and the like), then any time you write something about a customer, a prospect, a commitment you've made to yourself, an appointment you want to make, or something that happened; that you write it in that place and only in that place.

If you want to use a computer-based system, there are many fine systems. Some of them include: ACT!, Gold Mine, Maxximizer, and Sales Logix. There are legacy type systems created by companies like SAP, Oracle, and Siebel Systems. Finally, there are Internet based systems such as www.SalesForce.com, and www.SalesNet.com. By the time you read this, some of the ones I list might be obsolete, acquired by other companies, out of business, or have changed their names. That's OK. Just remember that the most important feature of computer-based systems is a contact management software program, also known as a "sales force automation program" or a "customer relations management (CRM) program." These are available in many formats from $99 to $999,999 or more.

If you decide to use a Web-based server to manage your time, the system will basically combine the alphabetical and chronological information for you. This means that anytime you bring up a record of a customer who is stored alphabetically and create a to-do item based on a time (such as "call Bob at 10:00 AM" or "meet with Warren for one hour on Tuesday, April 3"), a double entry is made for you in the alphabetical and chronological systems simultaneously. This is true whether you use a Web-based system or a computer-based system.

The only drawback to using a paper system is that you'll need to make the double entry yourself. Let's say, I'm using a paper system—I bring out my 8 1/2" by 11" manila folder and make notes in the file about the "Brown Company." Then I get Mr. Brown on the phone and he says, "Let's meet at 10:00 AM next Tuesday morning," and I write it only in the "Brown" file, then close the file and put it away behind the "B" tab.

I've just made a serious mistake. I've made no cross-reference to my chronological system. On the other hand, if I just take out my chronological paper system and I write down my appointment with "Mr. Brown" for 10:00 AM on April 3, I may not have all the information I need when I get to the appointment. I will also have not way to reference what happened before April 3rd.

Now you understand the benefit of having a system that enables you to work with both types of information at the same time. You keep the diary of what is committed to in the notes in the alphabetical file, then you simply make a note in the chronological file in terms of when you're going to take the next step with that particular client or prospect. In this way, when you get to the day known as April 3rd, and it says Brown at 10:00 AM, you simply go to the "Brown" file and all the notes are there.

This is the double entry bookkeeping system. You have to manage both the "What" (the alphabetical system), and the "When" (the chronological system).

SALES IDEA

SELF-MANAGEMENT

There are 24 hours in each day, 168 hours in every week. We all begin with the same quantity of time. Time cannot be saved, banked, delayed, or, I think, managed. This is why the concept of "managing time" is not the correct way of improving our productivity and enjoyment of life. Time moves forward relentlessly. It cannot be stopped.

Fortunately, there is a key element that is the essence of getting more done with less stress. It is the concept of self-management—the manner in which we manage *ourselves* plays a major role in how successful we are.

We are in charge of how we use our time. We can schedule activities that move our business ahead. We can delegate tasks to others. We can decide to eliminate certain things from our daily work. We can delay less important events and focus on what matters most.

What matters most as a sales professional are events that retain or service a client, expand a relationship with a current client, or find and land a new client. A blend of these three above actions is important to all of us.

Look at your calendar for this week. Notice how much time is committed to:

Item	Percent of time
servicing existing clients	
growing business from existing clients	
finding new clients	

(A good balance is 40–60 percent servicing, 10–30 percent growing, and 10–30 percent finding.)

Action: Rebalance your schedule for this week and *schedule activities* that will bring focus on retaining and growing your business. Remember: Scheduled activities drive out unscheduled activities.

The Distinction Between Urgent and Vital

It's very important for salespeople to recognize that they need to be driven by what's vital and not what is necessarily urgent. What I mean is that if there's a knock on the door or the phone rings, we have a tendency to react to it because it is urgent. We don't know if it's important or not. All we know is that it's urgent.

Too many times we're driven by the urgencies of the day, and we fail to get to do what's important. We react to the urgencies all day long and neglect the vital issues. An example of something that is important but not necessarily urgent might be a call to a prospect.

Think about it, this person isn't just sitting by the phone saying, "I hope Jill Jones calls from Office Equipment Specialties, because I'm really thinking of upgrading my printer network." Well, even if this prospect was thinking about upgrading the printing network, he or she has never heard of Jill Jones at Office Equipment Specialties, and so wouldn't be waiting around for our phone call.

So we might tend to deal with the current customers, get the proposals out, or do some research on the companies we're calling on, rather than make the prospecting call. There's no sense of urgency that says, "Make that phone call today!"

My goal is to make sure that you understand that the way to be successful in sales is to create your sense of urgency around what is vital.

ASK THE SALES DOCTOR

THE BEST TIME TO MAKE CALLS

Sally writes: "When is the best time to make initial prospecting and appointment-setting calls? I've been told to stay away from Monday mornings and Friday afternoons, as this is not a good time to be calling. What do you think?"

ANSWER

Sally, I'm really happy you sent this question in. You would not believe how many people in my seminars ask that question and say, "I've been told that Monday mornings and

Friday afternoons are bad times to call. What do you think?"

Well, Sally, that's a bunch of nonsense. It must have started during the 1950s. There was a misconception that "You shouldn't call on Monday morning because Mr. Business Executive is setting his schedule. And don't call on Friday afternoons because Mr. Business Executive is winding down the week and getting ready for the next week."

"Nobody wants to talk to salespeople on Monday mornings and Friday afternoons."

That's a bunch of bunk. Let me tell you the best time to make prospecting calls and initial approaches: *any time*. Let me give you some tips. Actually, Monday mornings are great times to call people because too many salespeople listened to those other tapes, read those other books, or went to those other seminars, and they're afraid to call on Monday mornings.

If people indeed are setting their calendars for the week, wouldn't that be the best time to call and get on those calendars? The answer is "Yes!" Monday mornings are a great time to set your agenda, set your calendar, and make appointment-setting calls.

And Friday afternoons are great times. Many times, a lot of the other people are leaving the office then, and those high-impact, high-energy decision-makers that you want to talk to are still working.

Let's take that one step further. If they're wrapping up their week and planning the next one, wouldn't that be a great time to be talking to them? The answer is "Yes!"

Here are some other great times to make initial prospecting and appointment-setting calls. If the business opens at 8:00, why not call somebody's direct extension at 7:42? Call them before everybody else is there; before the switchboard gets busy.

How about calling them at 11:59 AM or 12:03 PM when a lot of other people are going out to lunch? You would be shocked at how many decision-makers are sitting at their desks at 12:07 because they're trying to get things wrapped up. They don't have to punch a clock to go to lunch from 11:30–12:30 or 12:00–1:00. So try a couple of minutes before or a couple of minutes after when you think they might be going to lunch.

Another great time to call is after 5:00 PM. After all the business is done and everyone else is going home, the high level decision-maker is still at her desk. She doesn't want to fight rush hour traffic. She ends up working another hour or so, and then leaves her office after all the rush hour traffic is gone.

I've given you some ideas on when to call, but let me tell you something. Don't believe any of that stuff you've heard before about "bad times to call."

Bonus Answer

One other thing, if you're looking for the best time to talk to a particular individual, make a friend of the assistant to that person, or your referral source, then find out what that person's rhythms and routines are.

For example, I was attempting to reach a referred prospect of mine. I found out that this person comes in at noon and works till about midnight. So I never try calling him in the morning. I wait till after 5:00 in the afternoon, when I know he's got most of his crises out of the way.

He's been known as a really hard guy to get hold of. But I've never had a problem getting through to him, because I figured out what his schedule is and when is the best time to call him.

Urgent and Important Event Management

Urgent is the knock at the door. It is not necessarily important.

Important is what gets us to our goals. It is not necessarily urgent.

There are four categories of events in our lives:

1. *Important and Urgent.* We will do it right now every time. Examples:

A customer calls with an urgent request for you to accept an order and ship it overnight.

A prospect you have been trying to reach for the last two weeks calls you while you are in the middle of catching up on correspondence.

A customer who buys a small amount from you and who has the opportunity to buy a lot more has had a problem with a competitor and is calling you to see if you can help them out today.

2. *Urgent and not important.* A trap that distracts us from our goals that we need to learn to delegate or do later. Examples:

One of your manufacturer partners sends you new catalogs that replace the old catalogs and asks you to update your catalog information right away.

An unqualified prospect who has no money, no authority, and no need asks you numerous technical questions during a time that you have set aside to make outbound calls to excellent, qualified prospects.

A social call comes in to talk about last night's episode of a TV sitcom that you have no interest in hearing about.

3. *Important and not urgent.* Our best opportunity to enhance our productivity by creating a sense of urgency around the events that get us to our goals. Prospecting is in this category. Examples:

Launching one of your most important sales prospecting campaigns to an audience of new prospective customers with whom you have no natural referral network. This group represents enormous potential for you.

Sending out a referral letter to your ten best customers and asking them to give you information on fifteen specific companies that you have yet to do the research on.

Creating a strategic sales plan for the entire year for business that has broken down by product group, market share, revenue potential, and continues on into quarterly and monthly milestones and breakdowns.

4. *Not important and not urgent.* Time wasters we ought to eliminate from our lives.

Examples:

Below average salesperson that corners you by the copy machine to moan about how terrible life is.

A call that comes in from a person who got your name by accident and has no chance of ever buying from you who asked you to do some research to find him a group of companies that might be able to service his needs.

Checking one weeks worth of email that has been checked by your spam filter and that probably has not one iota of interest to you personally or professionally.

SALES IDEA

COMPLETE AN ACTION PLAN FOR ONE KEY PROSPECT

"Plan without action is FUTILE...action without plan is FATAL."
—Unknown

Write down one key prospect, create an account plan and then use that knowledge that you learned to go out and make a call on that person. Find a key prospect in your territory that you've been avoiding, neglecting or have been fearful about, and tell yourself that you are going to make a successful call on that potential customer.

I'm going to identify him or her strategically as someone who fits in my business. I'm going to write out my approach. I'm going to anticipate and overcome resistance. I'm going to go out there and knock on that door, or pick up the phone and make the call.

And I am going to find out what's going on with that prospect.

I'll tell you what: it works if you work. The key is to select not 10, not 52, not 73 prospects, but just select one. Find one prospect.

Action: Have a plan. Write out your approach. Make the call. And go out and see what happens.

Making Every Minute Count

The best way to make every minute count is to look at the items that you have previously scheduled into your day and act on them in terms of importance first and urgency second.

Remember that an *A* task is one that will move my business forward if I accomplish it; a *B* task is somewhat less important; and a *C* task is often a "Why bother?," but it's on the list anyway.

Making every minute count means that we do what is vital to move our business forward right now, not tomorrow or next week. We take those vital items in our day and we act upon them.

SALES IDEA

MAKING GOOD CHOICES—WORKING SMART
"There is no moment like the present."
—Edgeworth

How many times have we allowed ourselves to be dragged into situations that we know we should have walked away from?

Some examples include:

- working with a account who "bids and quotes" his business every year
- working with an account who invites multiple vendors into a bidding war
- working with an account that will not give us access to the decision-makers
- working on an account that is politically charged and we are not the connected supplier
- working on accounts where the revenue doesn't justify the work involved
- working on accounts where we don't have good solutions

We do this because we do not have enough of the "good stuff" in our universe of prospects. Panic sets in and we tend to work on anything that just shows up.

The Latin root of the word "decide" means to "cut yourself off from." Once we decide to work on better opportunities, we also decide *not* to work on the lesser opportunities.

Action: Choose to work on opportunities that give you the best chance at the type of successes that you know you can earn. Focus on people who see a value in you, who

aren't "bid and quote" oriented, who give you access to
decision makers and information, and who justify the time
and effort to which you will commit.

Rate your top five prospects in these areas and see how
they measure up. Are you working smart?

Be Like Mike

"A hero is one who knows how to hang on one minute
longer."—*Anonymous*

Think about Michael Jordan the basketball player, Larry Bird the
basketball player, or Tiger Woods the golfer. Every time you read
an article about them you find out that Michael Jordan was the first
one to practice and the last one there at the end of the day, Larry
Bird would throw a thousand free throws every day and Tiger
Woods has probably hit more golf balls than any fifty other golfers.

Why is this important? Because people who step up to the plate
and become excellent at their craft practice their business every day
on a consistent basis. What does this mean for salespeople?

Let's look at the actions that we need to do every day. We need
to:

- make outbound calls
- schedule appointments with qualified decision makers
- go to appointments and do an effective job of fact-finding
- do an exciting and enthusiastic job of presenting our company's offer
- ask for commitments
- follow up
- find out what's next

All these different issues are the fundamental skills for salespeople, just like dribbling, passing, rebounding, free throw shooting, and three-point shooting are important to basketball players. Just like driving, the short game and putting are important to golfers. We have to focus on the fundamentals and act on them on a daily basis. That's what being a professional salesperson is.

Be Like Einstein

In addition to being like Michael Jordan, "Like Mike", as the saying goes, we also want to be like Einstein in terms of being an effective self-manager. When he was asked late in his life why he was successful, Einstein didn't say, "Because I was a brilliant mathematician," or "Because my brain was bigger than anybody else's." He said, "The reason I've been successful in my life is that I have minimized the amount of time between hearing a good idea and acting upon that idea."

If you do research into the life of Thomas Edison you find out the same thing. He experimented over and over again. He certainly took the time to think

> **"Success or failure in business is caused more by mental attitude than by mental capacities."**
> —*Walter Dill Scott*

about things and daydream, but when the time came to act, he took action. He minimized the amount of time between hearing, seeing, or thinking about a good idea, and acting on it. When he was creating the light bulb he tried 999 different items that would light the electricity without burning out.

He finally found tungsten but he experimented with 999 different ways not to light a light bulb. He took action.

SALES IDEA

LOOK FOR AND ACT ON ONE IDEA EVERY DAY

Now the key phrase there is "act on." Let's say you are listening to an audio book or reading a sales book and you come upon a good idea. You might say, "Wow! What a great idea! One of these days I'm going to do that." Well, "one of these days" is not *acting now*.

In fact, it's been said that the difference between those who succeed greatly and those who don't is the time that elapses between receiving a good idea and acting on it. Remember Albert Einstein? He believed that to be true.

"Look for and act on one new idea every day", will be dynamic for you if you will do it every day. Here's my challenge: why don't you do it once? Why don't you do it today?

If there's something you've been meaning to do, do it. If there's a prospect you've been meaning to call on, then pick up the phone and call them.

Action: Do yourself a favor. Look for and act on one new idea every day.

Scheduled Activities Drive Out Unscheduled Activities

When I first heard a statement similar to this, I was astounded by how effective that phrase became for me. Too many times we allow the day to control us—instead of us controlling the day. We let the time slip through our fingers like sand through our fingers at the beach, or through the hour glass. In order for us to maximize our day, we have to find out what's important to us, and we have to schedule it just like we would schedule a massage, or dinner with a friend. We need to schedule those activities that help move our business forward.

To repeat, the activities that are important to us are making it happen, picking up the phone, making the call, scheduling the prospecting time, getting the new appointments with new prospects and inactive customers, finding out what their needs are, developing solutions and then asking for and receiving commitments.

We have to schedule those activities and that forces out some of the lower-priority activities that we find ourselves doing. As my friend Rob Lowry said to me, "We have to schedule our priorities rather than prioritize our schedule." That's brilliance.

This is the hallmark of how I've lived my life in sales and life in general for many, many years. Most people focus on the urgent and not the important. When we do this we do the items on our To Do List that are either the easiest to do or don't take much time. Those larger items such as developing our new business, making sure we're talking to the right people at the right companies, or working on a strategy for a particular account—they all go by the wayside as we go from one crisis to the next.

Again, scheduled activities drive out unscheduled activities. If we understand that, put pencil to paper, and say, "I'm going to carve out this two-hour block to work on this project," it's much more likely to happen than if we just think about it, dream about it, wish about it, or hope about it. Because scheduled activities drive out unscheduled activities.

ASK THE SALES DOCTOR

QUESTION
Priscilla, writing from Anchorage, says, "I have an excellent memory. Why do you suggest that I write everything down when I'm on calls with my customers?"

ANSWER

What happens if you are in a meeting with a customer and they give you a task list of maybe five to seven items and you're remembering them as you walk out of their office, then as soon as the door closes behind you the phone rings and there is a client emergency across town, followed by a service outage at another customer, followed by a traffic jam, followed by your child having a problem at his school, and followed by your spouse telling you he or she will be late? Do you think after all that stress that you would remember the five to seven items the customer and you talked about? I doubt it. Why spend all that mental memory trying to remember some of these details? Why not just write them down so you can fill your mind with the things that make a difference, instead of the day-to-day details that you can forget about once you accomplish them.

How to Diagnose our Sales Illnesses and Treat Ourselves to the Correct Cures

Salespeople can diagnose their own illnesses. It's quite simple once we understand how to measure our own sales metrics. If we are not bringing enough business in the door, we have to ask ourselves, "Are we asking for enough commitments?"

When we measure the statistic of how many commitments we have asked for and how many commitments we have received, then we will know whether we're effective at working with resistance. If you ask ten people to do business and only one says "Yes" and nine say "No" or "Not yet," then you know you have an issue. Your illness is that you're not able to work through resistance or you're not asking for the business in the right way.

If we are not bringing enough business in the door to meet quota, and our ratio of asking for commitments to receiving commitments is above 33 percent, then we're way above average. If we're still not making our number then the question is—to how many people are we asking the question? And that would usually be a function of our illnesses, meaning that we don't have enough people in the pipeline.

And again, that could be diagnosed and worked with by understanding how to measure our own statistics. We can absolutely understand what our illnesses are and cure ourselves. On the front end of the sales process, if we're making 15 outbound calls per hour and only getting through to one decision-maker per hour, then obviously we have an issue of getting through. The average ought to be close to 33 percent.

If we make 15 outbound calls we ought to be able to get through to five people. Now if you get through to five people and you have no appointments, there's another problem we need to overcome. We are not asking for the appointment over the phone. We are trying to find too much on the phone. Instead of using it for an appointment-setting tool, we are trying use it for a sales tool. If we are in face-to-face selling this is another inappropriate use and another illness we can fix.

The point here is that once we understand how to measure our sales metrics we can diagnose and cure any illness. Okay. Let's take stock now and see where we are. This entire discussion about self-management for sales professionals sounds so completely natural and so obvious that the question ought to be: Doesn't everybody do this? The answer is a resounding no. This is an area that has a tremendous payback if we implement the ideas as I presented them in this section of the book. The total salesperson begins to realize and always has in his or her awareness that the three principles—sales process, sales plan and sales practice—are interactive and interdependent. Sales practice is the finishing touch on making sure that we are going to reach our sales goals and have a lot of fun while we are on this journey of selling excellence.

Chapter Eight

Effective Sales Practice in Action

"Nothing is particularly hard if you divide it into small jobs."—*Henry Ford*

When all is said and done, we have to realize that what we are paid to do in the world of sales is not really completely based on our productivity. Bear with me here. We aren't really paid on how many new accounts we opened, how many sales we brought in the door, whether we reached quota, what our revenue was for the year, or what our gross profit was. Let me explain.

The above statements are all examples of "lagging indicators." They are the result of the activities that preceded them. The true essence of being successful in selling is to focus on *activities* daily. When we focus on doing the right activities based on a sound strategic sales plan, and when we utilize the best practices of self-management to make these things happen on a daily basis, then we can guarantee that the productivity will be there later. Productivity is a lagging indicator.

Activity Leads to Productivity

> "Life is a mirror; if you frown at it, it frowns back; if you smile, it returns the greeting."
> —*Thackeray*

Activity leads to productivity. It's a great habit. That's why I emphasize activity when I'm working with new or experienced salespeople. Now, understand that I'm also making sure there is a very sound sales plan and that these people have a measurable and repeatable sales process to follow. But when everything is all said and done, the people who are most successful are those who take action. This is how I help new people get going in the right direction quickly.

Account Activity the Right Way

Now let's look at how we're going to schedule our time, based on spending the perfect amount of time with the perfect opportunities. First we have to review some concepts that were presented earlier. As we discussed, a total salesperson has three fundamental jobs to do. First, the salesperson retains current business. Second, the salesperson grows the business he has. Third, the salesperson looks for and brings in new business opportunities. When taken together, these three ideas are what create a secure present and future for the total salesperson.

Another concept we've talked a lot about is making sure we spend the right amount of time on the proper activity. Now we also know that the proper activity inevitably leads to the productivity we all are striving for. The productivity aspect is reaching our goals based on our sales plan. Now you see how all the concepts work together. In order for us to understand the action based on these above ideas, we have to really leverage the self-management concepts we've developed earlier in this chapter and make absolutely sure that, in any given moment, we are doing the absolute correct thing based on that moment in time. This is account activity the right way.

Sales Practice for A and B Accounts For our *A* and *B* accounts, that is, those accounts that are already doing a significant amount of business with us or have the potential to be doing a lot, we have to ask ourselves three questions. The first question is: How do we intend to retain the business we have? That means doing things like:

- working with the organization to make sure we have a relationship with all the decision makers
- understanding who the competition is and how active they are in the account
- knowing what the strategic direction is with this particular customer
- knowing whether or not this customer is happy with our service
- knowing what type of road blocks we've put in the way of doing business
- knowing what we can do to make business easier for both of us
- asking them questions about what we can be doing more of to make sure that business continues to come our way.

The second question: How do we intend to grow this account? This is a very simple yet profound exercise that I suggest to many of my clients. First, take out a sheet of paper and write

> **"Some men have thousands of reasons why they cannot do what they want to, when all they need is one reason why they can."**
> —*Mary Frances Berry*

down on one side all the different types of products or services this particular customer buys from you. On the other side of the page, write down all the products and services other customers like this one might buy.

Next, simply introduce new ideas from the "other side of the page" every single time you meet with that customer to let them know what you have in terms of ideas that can help them move their business forward, save them time, save them money, make it a more safe environment for their associates, enhance moral, reduce turnover, and so on.

The third question we need to ask all of our *A* and *B* accounts is: What type of referral opportunities might there be for us to work either more closely with their company or with their companies that they know and we do not? That is the essence of referrals—finding out people they know who we don't know and getting introductions.

Sales Practice for C Accounts For *C* accounts our focus is a bit different. By the way, you might wonder why we even call on *C* accounts. As mentioned earlier, the answer is that we want to farm the *C* account base to look for tomorrow's *A* and *B* accounts.

Now, with this group, we would ask ourselves questions like: "What are our initial approach ideas and why would they want to meet with us in the first place?" If they are *C* accounts, they may not know much about us. They have suppliers that they are currently buying from, so we need to make sure that we know what we're going to say when we approach them.

The next question we need to ask is: What is our lead-in and what are we going to say to get them to at least meet with us, share ideas with us, or even answer questions that would disqualify them from working with us? (Such as: they're too small, they're always going to be too small, or they've got a brother-in-law type relationship with one of our competitors that we could never break through. These are questions we need to ask to determine if ever are going to be able to move those *C* accounts into *A* or *B* status.

Another question we need to ask is: What are our ideas to gain market share? A good way to help answer this question is to ask: Who are the weakest competitors that are currently doing business with them? You know, they say that a chain is only as strong as its weakest link. Why go after your strongest, fiercest competitor when it's a lot easier to pick off the weak competitors?

Now you might say, "Warren, isn't that a predatory way to think about your business?" The answer is yes. I always go after my weakest competitors first. That builds my credibility and my clout with my *C* accounts and positions me to go after the tougher competitors next.

Finally, maybe the reason some of our customers are *C* accounts is because we're not talking to the right people. So the final question we need to ask is: What additional decision-makers do we need to meet to break through some resistance? After all, if you're not getting a whole lot of business from a company, there is very little risk in meeting someone new. You may be dealing with a decision-influencer rather than a decision-maker, and you want to get to the people who can actually make things happen.

ASK THE SALES DOCTOR

QUESTION
Beverly, a friend of mine and a skeptic, asks, "Warren, you say that C accounts should receive an unfair share of our time, meaning that we should spend more of our time with our A and B accounts. How do you know that C account won't become tomorrows A and B account?"

ANSWER
I've heard this comment a hundred times and a hundred

times I've been right when I say that you are going to get more business from those *A* and *B* accounts. It's like the story about Willie Sutton the bank robber. When he was asked, "Why did you rob all those banks?" he replied, "Because that's where the money was." The same thing is true in sales. The only reason we have any *C* accounts is that maybe 1 or 2 percent of those over time will rise into the ranks of *A* and *B* accounts. If I knew that I could generate the type of growth I wanted for my business by only calling on *A* and *B* accounts, I would never, ever call an account that was anything less than an *A* or *B*. Believe me when I tell you that 70 to 80 percent of your time ought to be spent with 20 to 30 percent or your accounts. The exception proves the rule and that is why you have an occasional *C* account that rises to *A* or *B* status. There will be that miracle where someone starts working in their garage and they build the next Apple computer. It's very, very rare.

Frequency of Contact I'm always asked how often we should call on customers. When I worked with a salesperson years ago, I asked him. "Where are we going today and why?" His response was, "Today is Tuesday, and here is my Tuesday schedule." I noticed that he was calling on many small accounts that really never had amounted to much and probably never would. In my book, they were *C* accounts.

"Little by little makes a cup full."
—*Unknown*

My question to him was, "Why do you call on these people every week? He really didn't have a good answer. If you know that the customer has only bought a small amount for the last ten years and they are a modest player and they will always purchase a little of your product for the next ten years, why call on that customer every week? Why not ask that customer, "How often do you think I should call on you? Would it be OK if I made one face-to-face visit per month and then made phone appointments with 20 percent once per month?" When the salesperson implemented this particular strategy of asking the customer to tell him how often they wanted to be called, it was amazing how much time he gained.

And what did he do with the time? He went after those inactive *A* and *B* prospective accounts or prospected accounts that he never had time to call on before. He had been driving by dollars to pick up dimes.

SALES IDEA

KEEPING SCORE

Too often in sales, we are overly focused and concerned about making the sale. There is a tendency to concentrate on final outcomes, booked revenue, percent at, ahead and behind plan, and the like. These are important issues, yet they only tell part of the story.

These are productivity factors—revenue booked, new account opened, products sold—they are the results that we desire.

While the end game or result is certainly important, it is a lagging indicator. The true measure of the future success of our business is to be found in understanding and tracking *activities*. Here is a rule of successful selling: Activity leads to productivity. The activities that will give us the best picture of our future business are:

- dials or new approaches
- decision-makers contacted

- initial appointments made or subsequent appointments set
Understand and leverage the 10-3-1 rule. In business-to-business sales, when we make ten dials, we will get through to three people and set one appointment.

Here is another number we can track. In one hour of uninterrupted outbound dialing, a salesperson will make ten to fifteen dials. Therefore, a salesperson ought to be able to arrange one appointment per hour of uninterrupted outbound dialing.

Action: Focusing on the right activities can be as important as productivity. Schedule three one-hour outbound dialing sessions and track statistics.

A simple 4 x 6 index card next to their phone is all you need.

"The ultimate measure of a man is not where he stands in moments of comfort and convenience, but where he stands at times of challenge and controversy."
—*Martin Luther King Jr.*

Being Persistent Without Being a Pest There are many stories that I could tell from my own sales career and those of people whom I have counseled over the years about the distinction between being a persistent salesperson and being a pest. In fact, recently I met with one of my customers and a group of us was talking about how it is so important to be persistent and consistent in pursuing business opportunities that make sense for both the account and for our companies.

One of the salespeople in the meeting asked me, "How often is too often and when should we give up?" My response was that if the account has *A* or *B* potential, then we never give up. We call on that account relentlessly, persistently, and consistently until that account actually starts giving us some business or tells us no, and it's the final answer.

Mind you, the negative response rarely occurs. Most of the time, by being persistent and consistent, we can actually grow business pretty significantly.

Someone else said, "Yes, we had a relationship with a particular vendor and a competitive supplier had been calling on us every month for about two years. We kept telling him, 'We already have a relationship, we're not going to change the relationship, and you're wasting your time.' The representative responded, "I don't want to be a pest. I just want to let you know we're out here, some things might change, and one of these days you might be looking for a different supplier—and I just want you to know I can help you if that ever happens."

As it turned out, the incumbent go-to supplier changed its policy and in fact wasn't able to deliver on their promises as they had in the past. So who do you think my customer called as soon as they could make a move? Of course, they called the person that had been calling on them persistently over the last two years.

So we always have to ask ourselves the question: Are we being persistent without crossing that line? In fact, over the years that I've walked a fine line between being persistent and being a pest. I want people to know that I want to earn their right to your business and I will be persistent in a persuasive and consistent manner. If I ever cross that line and become a pest, I ask them to let me know right away. It's never happened.

ASK THE SALES DOCTOR

QUESTION

Chris writes, "It seems to me that I make an awful lot of calls to get very few appointments. Why do you think that is?"

ANSWER

In my experience, most people who fail to secure a decent amount of appointments have a flawed approach. The flaw is that instead of seeking out the appointment on the initial call, the person is spending way too much time trying to sell the product or service instead of selling the appointment. If we stay focused on the objective, which is to get the appointment and at every opportunity to have the conversation to go in a different area, we instead say, "That's a great point and when I meet with you we will have a chance to talk about that," or, "That's a great question and I'll answer that when we meet face-to-face." Then ask the person, "How about next Tuesday at 3:00 or how about Monday morning?" You will find that just being *that* committed to the appointment will help you improve your ratio.

Launching Our Prospecting Campaigns I'm a big believer in focused attention because what we place our attention on grows stronger. This is perfectly applicable to the way we go about launching our prospecting campaigns. In my view, too many of us spend too much energy calling on too many people. We ought to reduce the amount of effort we put into the shotgun approach and instead have a series of tightly focused sales campaigns.

I suggest that we have no more than four and no fewer than three campaigns going on at any given time. Here are some examples:

- growth campaigns to current customers
- retention campaigns to current customers
- geographic campaigns into a new area that we would like to develop

Campaigns can also be built around a particular product or service that we offer, they can be referral campaigns, or they can be center-of-influence campaigns. There are so many that we could launch. My point is that we do three to four campaigns at a time and focus on them for thirty, sixty, or ninety days or up to six months at a time before we change to a new series of campaigns.

Scheduling Account Reviews

It's very important to spend the time finding out from your customer base if you're doing the right or the wrong things, where the opportunities are for growth, and where you may be at risk in the future. I suggest that you conduct account reviews once per quarter with your *A* and *B* customers. This account review ought to contain some very specific actions.

First, you should thank the customer for the business they have given you over the last month, quarter, or year—mention the specific business. Bring reports, show them what they're buying from you, and tell them how much you appreciate it.

Next, offer the customer ideas on how to better utilize your products and services. There might be better ways for them to buy in terms of quantities or frequency. There could be different products or services that you provide that are actually a better fit for this customer. When you have a chance to look at the last quarter, month, or year's worth of purchases, you can be more strategic with them.

Third, get further into a strategic discussion. Ask questions such as:

- What is your company's strategic plan?
- What are your company's business initiatives for this year?

- What's important to you?
- What are the most challenging issues your business is facing?
- What type of competitive pressures are you under in your business that are causing you concerns?
- What are some of the issues of the day that your industry-specific trade publications are telling you are items that you ought to be thinking about in your business today?

Really focus strategically to discover what's important to them and how your companies match up.

The next part of the account review is to probe for new or additional needs. Ask questions like:

- Are there some areas that wake you up screaming at 3:00 in the morning because of a glitch with another vendor?
- How can we serve you better?

Instead of launching into a tirade against the competition or a soliloquy about how wonderful your new products or services are, you might find out that you're trying to sell meat to vegetarians, and that wouldn't work. Why not ask the customer? That's why the third part of this review probes for new or additional needs. Ask the customer open-ended questions.

Finally, based on what goes on during the first parts of the meeting, you should now present new ideas. Show them the direction that your company is going and let them know the exciting things you are doing to maintain and grow your business with them. Show them new ways to utilize your products and services to create value for them. Demonstrate how they can save time, streamline their business, reduce errors, eliminate hassles or add profit to their bottom line. And, because you've spent so much time talking about their needs earlier in the discussions, they're much more open to listen to what is new at your company.

This is the essence of account review, and it's critically important for salespeople to do it.

SALES IDEA

GROWING THROUGH ADD-ON SALES MADE EASY AS A CAMPAIGN

An easy way to determine other suggestions you can make to a customer is to take out a sheet of paper and on the left side write down all the products and services that a particular client buys from you. Then on the right side of the paper write down what your best customers in that same industry buy. If you don't have a customer that's a perfect fit, just use the one who's the closest match. If a particular customer in that business bought everything from you, what would be on the right side of the page? You will amaze yourself at how many times the right side is two, three, or four times the length of what's on the left side. This proves to us that the add-on and cross-sell are an underutilized yet effective way to grow business.

Action: Do this exercise for your best three accounts.

Self-Management the Right Way

Let's put self-management in the proper perspective. The sales plan is the guide for all of our daily actions. The sales process is the method that we use to implement the sales plan. Sales practice, the topic of this chapter, encompasses the tactics we use to carry out the methods. Self-management can be perceived, incorrectly, as micromanagement. This is the wrong way to view it. It can also be viewed, incorrectly, as "big brother looking over your shoulder." This is also incorrect. The reason it's so important for all of us as sales professionals, as Total Salespeople, to understand what we're doing on a year-by-year, quarter-by-quarter, month-by-month, week-by-week, day-by-day, and heck even sometimes hour-by-hour, basis is that it's the only way to leverage the ideas of sales process and sales plan effectively.

If you don't know that what you're doing at this moment is focused on one aspect of the sales process that is directly correlated to your sales plan, then you are not going to be as successful as you might be if everything was tied together. That's self-management the right way. Monitoring activities the right way is closely aligned with the idea of self-management the right way. There's an expression "If it is to be, it's up to me." As much as people within our organization care about our performance and about our appropriate level of activity, when it comes right down to it, no one cares as much about our relative success as we do. Unless you have a direct one-on-one relationship with the person with whom you work most closely, you are not in the other person's awareness at every moment. *You* are the only person who can honestly and seriously look at what you are doing every day and compare it to what you know you ought to be doing in order to attain the level of success that you have put forward when you wrote your sales plan. The best way to do this is to understand what the sales metrics are that make your business go and then measure and monitor your performance on a regular basis.

Creating an Ideal Day, Week, Month, Quarter, or Year It is also important for us to understand what we should be working on at any given time, and I believe in working the equation both ways. On one hand, I want to make sure I'm maximizing my efforts every day to make sure I'm doing the right activities to lead to my long-term productivity. On the other hand, I want to look at the big picture to make sure that I am focused on the long term, and I understand that the long term is just a series of short terms. So I work both ends against the middle.

I always look at the long term, big picture so I know why I'm doing the things I'm doing. Then I look at the short term, asking myself, "What am I doing today?" The *what* and the *how* will help me get to the *why*. I am a big believer in trying to make each day an ideal day, and I schedule as much action and activity into my day as possible. However, I'm after long-term productivity, and I can't be so rigid that I have no time for creativity and flexibility.

It's a balancing act between scheduling activities and giving myself free time to be able to react when new opportunities come my way.

Once mastered, two techniques, the look-forward and the look-back, can greatly help you achieve sales success. Here's why.

The Look Back We need to stop the clock on a regular basis to find out how effectively we're moving our business in the direction we want it to go. This is called a "look back." The best way to do this is to schedule time every Friday afternoon to stop the clock and look back over the last week with your goals in front of you. Compare your big-picture goals with what you've actually accomplished during the week.

You will shock yourself at how many times you felt good during the week about being busy, but when you look at long-term goals, you realize you didn't do one thing to move your business forward. You confused "any" activity with the "right" activity. That is a bad thing.

The reason you should do this look back every week is that the maximum amount of time that can go by in which you're off the track is one week. So that's what a look back is. You look back over one week, compare your actual performance and activities to the goals you have set for the month, quarter, year and you compare the big picture to the little picture.

The Look Forward Now, at that same time on Friday, you look forward one week. Look at your calendar, your appointments, your tasks, and your to-do list to see how many of those items are leading you toward your longer-term goals. Again, you will shock yourself at how many times you've confused busy work with the activities that will move your business forward.

It's good to engage with another person in this weekly review. That person may be a buddy, a mentor, an associate, or even your sales leader. Look at your upcoming week again and schedule items into our day that help you move toward your long-term goals.

The importance of look back and look forward cannot be overemphasized. Too many people do not do this, yet it's one of the major things I recommend when I counsel individual salespeople.

Monitoring Activities the Right Way

Sales Metrics Why is it so important therefore to keep score? Because when you add up the razor-thin chance of error or success in selling, the high volume of calls that need to be made, the high level of rejection that salespeople encounter, it's important to know exactly what's going on: how many calls are being made, what's being said, and how that customer responded. We need to do everything in our power to increase the ratios of successful outcomes to the corresponding activities.

It is important to understand what statistics you need to measure and why. This statistical approach I'm going to share with you occurs no matter what environment you're working in. If you're a new business selling a new product or if you're already a current supplier assigned to current customers, the same statistics apply.

First, you need a way to track activities. You can create an Excel spreadsheet. You could do the same thing using one of the contact management programs like Act or Goldmine. You could do it based on using sheets of paper or 4 x 6 index cards. I don't care how you do it—as long as you do it. It is important that you monitor the following statistics. Bear with me because I am going to share a lot of information with you, but it's all very important.

On a day-by-day basis, what we want to track is a whole range of statistics. The first one is called Attempts, Dials, or Approaches. If you're doing all the work by phone, then call it dials. How many times a day, a half-day, or an hour do you actually pick up the phone and dial a number? The second statistic we want to track is Contacts Made or Decision-Makers Reached. When you have these two statistics, you have an opportunity to make a comparison.

These first two statistics, when looked at together, are very important. Why? If I pick up the phone, dial it fifty times, and get through to two decision-makers, do you think I need help in what I'm saying, how to work with receptionists, how to make sure you're not treating them like "rejectionists," gatekeepers, or screeners? The answer is yes; the average in most major metropolitan areas is that you will get through to about one-third of the people you dial. This means if you dial sixty people, you'll get through to twenty of them.

Do you see why it's so important to be able to keep score and have statistics to measure, to have the information you need to track, how to track it, and what all these different activities and ratios mean? You can diagnose your own sales issues, or if you're a sales manager who's looking at the statistics from your sales group, you have an opportunity to find out exactly where you can help your salespeople.

The next statistic I like to measure is called Appointments Set. This is where you're using the phone to make the initial face-to-face appointment. It's important to understand that if you contact ten decision-makers and you get no appointments, you are likely trying to sell your *product* or *service* over the phone instead of offering or selling the *appointment*. The general rule with this statistic is that if you contact ten people, you ought to be able to set appointments with three of them, about one-third. This means that 70 percent of the time you're going to be rejected.

The next statistic I like to track is called Needs Identified. That simply means that you're entering into a dialogue with the prospect to start asking him about his current situation, what his needs are, what he likes and doesn't like, what he would need in a new product or service. If you're looking at "Decision-Makers Contacted, 10 and Needs Identified, 0," that tells me as one who understands statistics that you're not asking questions. You're going right from contacting the decision-maker to "pitching" your solution.

The next category is called Solutions Presented. This means that once you have identified the needs and you have asked this person a lot of questions, it's time to make the bridge to present your solution. If you contact ten people and you have a chance to identify the needs of five, you'd better have five solutions presented. Once you've identified their needs, you have to take that transition step and start showing them how your product or service fits in with the needs you've identified.

The next statistic is the most important of all and that's called Commitments Asked For. Too many people just keep talking and never stop to ask somebody if they want to buy, if they're interested, or how they're doing so far. If I go through a whole list of calls that someone's made and realize that they're not asking anybody to do anything, I realize they need help in learning how to ask obligating questions.

The next statistic is called Commitments Received. If you ask ten people for the order and you only get 1 to say yes, I'd go back to the quality of your questions because one out of ten is an unacceptable percentage of people buying out of people who are asked to buy. The average salesperson usually gets two or three out of ten, or 20 to 30 percent out of ten, and top salespeople can move that number up to 50 percent or more. So again, do you see why it's so important to have these statistics that are laid out, that are measurable?

This is what I call keeping score of the selling game.

SALES IDEA

MAKE YOUR NEXT CALL YOUR BEST CALL

Many salespeople save their best calls for tomorrow, yet tomorrow never comes. Many salespeople feel that when they finally get around to making the best call they are a "day late and a dollar short." The best way to overcome this habit is to make the next call the best call. Write down the name of your very best prospect. It could be a current account that you want to sell additional services to, an inactive account that you want to re-establish a relationship with, or a brand new prospect that you are calling for the very first time. Next, commit to approaching your best prospect before you do anything else! (and before your fiercest competitor does it before you!)

Action: Make the call now. Do it now. Don't hesitate. Take action.

Sales Metrics in Action I'd been working with a new client for about two weeks. They had been monitoring their statistics for ten days. Interestingly enough, the president of the company is someone I've known for a number of years and worked with on numerous projects. I know how he thinks, and he knows how I think. He knew, for example, that I was going to talk to all the salespeople one-on-one. I had phone conferences scheduled every fifteen minutes with a salesperson. I was looking at the statistics. I knew what the problems were. I knew how to diagnosis their issues. So in that fifteen-minute conversation I could do a lot of coaching and redirecting of energy with all these various salespeople. The night before I was to make these calls, I got an email from the president of the company. He had been looking at the same statistics I had been looking at, and he said, "When you talk to Bob, ask him why or how he's getting through to 60 percent of the people, which we both know is above average. And when you talk to Sally ask her how she is finding so many people who are interested compared to the rest of us who are only finding maybe one out of fifty. How come Sally is getting three out of forty."

So he went through each statistic. He and I both know what the standard ratios are. He was able to point out areas of great need as well as areas of great strength. So when I got a chance to talk to the individuals, I could find out what they were doing well and I could work that into the rest of the people's calls. Later, we brought them into a group meeting so they could share with each other what they'd been doing, and have them highlight their strengths and weaknesses.

I have just shared with you the best diagnostic tools for sales-people—and it's called keeping score, knowing what and how to track, putting it all together, seeing what it all means in terms of activities and ratios, and then knowing how to diagnose your own sales issues.

Final Thoughts

Congratulations! You have mastered Total Selling. You are now a total salesperson. In fact, if I were with you right now, and I had a lapel pin handy, I would annoint you as a CTS—Certified Total Salesperson. Why? Because you have learned the three fundamental principals behind this powerfully simple yet profound idea. You have created your own sales process. You have created a sales plan. And you have learned the sales practice that will guarantee your success. You have now joined the ranks of the very few salespeople who understand the why, the what, and the how of what it takes to rise to the top in profession of selling. You know why you do the things you do because you have a great sales plan. You know what you're supposed to be doing everyday because you have identified and implemented your own sales process. And you know how to go about your tasks because you utilize effective sales practice daily. So again, congratulations and great work!

Chapter Nine

Afterword: The Total Selling Mindset

Becoming the Best We Can Be

Based on the ideas in the previous section, I imagine you're pretty pumped up about your ability to be successful once you unlock the keys to your own motivation. Are you willing to take the next step and look at some additional concepts that will greatly determine how truly successful you really can be? If the answer is yes, then keep reading because I'm about to share with you some potentially thought-provoking ideas that I have noticed over the years in my career and the careers of the thousands of people with whom I've worked. These ideas have made a tremendous amount of difference in the lives of the sales professionals with whom I've shared them. First, I will discuss these strategies, and then I will wrap up the afterword—and the book—by analyzing *motivation*.

Some of these ideas might make you uncomfortable. In fact, try this right now. Cross your arms the way you have always crossed them your whole life and notice how that feels. If you're like most people, it feels pretty comfortable. Now, uncross your arms and cross them the opposite way—put the arm that was on the top on bottom and arm that was on the bottom on the top—and notice how that feels. If you're like 99 percent of the people who I've done this exercise with, you're quite uncomfortable. Change is uncomfortable. That's a fact. As you look over this list that you are about to read in terms of ways to become your best and you feel like you could do more or be better or make a change, understand that there might be some discomfort. Growth can be painful, however, growth is always rewarding. Are you ready? Let's go!

Reasonableness

Life is all about transformations. For instance, sometimes it's important *not* to be reasonable; it's better to be unreasonable. Reasonable may mean, "I'm trying hard, I'm making good reasonable decisions, I did my best" and all that—but sometimes you have to step beyond reasonableness and become unreasonable. You have to do better; you have to decide that the valid reason for not being successful up to this point is just not good enough, and you have to be unreasonable. Unreasonably disciplined, unreasonably hard working, unreasonably daring, unreasonably out of the ordinary, unreasonably thinking outside of the box. It means not saying, "I did my best" but saying, "I am doing whatever it takes to get things done."

Integrity

Integrity means, "I am my word." Life is all about honesty, trust, and integrity, and we have to be true to our own selves and in tune with our own values. Also, if we make promises, we need to keep them. It's interesting that integrity is something that is a hallmark of so many religious philosophies.

For instance, the main theme of Yom Kippur, the Day of Atonement (the holiest day within the Jewish faith), focuses on the promises that were made and broken to friends, others, and God.

We are to atone for our broken vows and complete our promises. It is of the utmost importance to keep our promises—to have integrity.

Breakthroughs

To live an extraordinary life, which we would all like to do, involves a series of breakthroughs. "Breakthrough" is an interesting play on words. A breakthrough is just that—breaking through. It's deciding to do something that is strong as opposed to just letting things happen.

There are three kinds of people in the world; those that let things happen (those are the re-actives), those that make things happen (those are the pro-actives), and those that wonder what the heck happened (those are the in-actives).

In order to live an extraordinary life, we have to really push ourselves to have a series of breakthroughs. We have to be willing to take that risk to knock on the doors, to open up our mind to new opportunities and new possibilities. Hence, when we breakthrough resistance we can maximize ourselves. We make things happen.

The Latin root of "decide" means "to cut away from." So what that means is that when you decide to do one thing, you're cutting yourself off from all other opportunities. It takes a very strong will, a strong mind, and determination to be able to break through and to be able to decide and to choose.

Responsible

You have to be responsible for yourself *and* others. Many people, though, don't want to take responsibility for their actions. They wonder why they get certain consequences. Yet when the progression is quite clear—actions lead to consequences. Actions Become Consequences. Easy as A, B, C.

If you are pondering a certain consequence, look at your actions that brought you to that consequence. If you're overweight and out of shape, that's the consequence. What's the action? You're sitting in front of the TV, you're not eating right, you're not exercising, and you're basically not doing the right actions.

Any consequence you can ever imagine, from being overweight, to not having the career you want, to being depressed, to being unfulfilled, is based on actions. It's the input that determines the output. That's why it's so important for us to be responsible, to make good choices based on being responsible to ourselves.

When The Going Gets Tough, The Tough Start Selling

Business is slow. The economy is in a recession. The phones aren't ringing. Does this sound like you? Are you tired of hearing this? Would you like to know how to deal with it? Read on. Remember: Nothing happens until somebody sells something. This simple yet powerful statement is more true today than ever before. It seems counterintuitive to be more aggressive in our selling activities when times are slow. Most salespeople and companies are happy enough just to hold on to the business they have, let alone take a risk in attempting to find new business. Yet, this is exactly what we need to be doing when times are slow. To model the Marines, when the going gets tough, the tough salespeople start selling.

What is Motivation?

What is "motivation"? A lot of people use that word, but they don't even know what it means.

My definition of motivation is: Something that encourages you or makes you take action. What's underlying what you're trying to accomplish in your life? Once you figure out what that purpose is, or what's meaningful to you, then you will take action. So the motivation is the underlying cause of the actions we take in our lives.

A pet peeve of mine concerns so-called motivational speakers.

Their goal is to pull from some external source something that's going to pump people up and get them to take action.

The problem I've always had with motivational speakers is that they're like a tire pump and you're like a flat tire needing air. While you're there, they'll pump you up and get you all filled with air, but at the end of the speech, they take their pump with them. If you've got a nail hole in your tire, or if you're not ready to take over pumping up that tire on your own, then you're going to quickly go as flat as you were before, maybe even flatter.

So the risk we run when we look to others for motivation is that it becomes a wild ride with lots of ups and downs. The key is to think about what is going to motivate *you*, because only *you* can motivate yourself.

Think about inspiration as opposed to motivation. Consider people who have overcome great odds—people who were born with a missing limb, completely blind, or some other misfortune—and despite them, were able to achieve great success. Many times, you look at the media or go to programs or seminars, and you see people who have overcome terrible things that happened in their lives—and that's supposed to motivate us.

We feel guilty. We think, "Oh, well, gee whiz, that person was born into poverty, abused when he was young, in a car accident and laid up for three years, and then got depressed afterward." And then you say, "Oh, look at all the things he's had to overcome. I'm pretty normal. I should be able to do that as well. I'm a loser by comparison."

The problem is that we tend to compare ourselves to other people instead of looking within. If you look around at any given place, most of the people are just like you and you're just like them. I call it being super-ordinary. Most of us are not extra-ordinary, although I think we each have a unique set of skills. But, generally, we're all basically the same—every man, every woman. So I don't think that motivational stories from people that overcame great odds to be successful will necessarily motivate us.

So what does work? It's all about motivation from within. Let's examine how we access our own unique and special reasons to succeed.

A Sense of Purpose

The first component of motivation is having a sense of purpose. In other words, you have an idea in your heart that you can do something, impact other people, and make a difference.

For example, in my business, I am dedicated to helping improve every single person in the world who considers him or herself a salesperson and is willing to work hard at self-improvement. That means if you're a direct salesperson, supporting a salesperson, managing a salesperson, a small business owner, an entrepreneur and you have to sell your product or service in order for your business to thrive, I'm here for you.

My sense of purpose is that if I successfully share my knowledge about the sales profession, I will be doing something good for other people—I can have an impact. I can make a difference in the lives of people who sell for a living.

My question to you is: What's your sense of purpose? If you're in the real estate business, for example, you might have a sense of purpose to help the people you work with choose the best housing alternatives, to live the lifestyle that they want—a great home in a safe neighborhood for their children to grow up in, appliances that work, and a neighborhood where they'll be able to see some appreciation when they sell.

Ask yourself: What is my sense of purpose? Do I have one?

Believe in You

The second component of motivation is to believe in you. You must really believe in yourself and your company. For example, if you're in the industrial distribution business and you don't believe that your company provides the best possible products, service, warranties, guarantees, knowledge, and competitive prices, then the first time someone approaches you and gives you some type of resistance or obstacle, you're going to fold up your tent. You're not going to know what to say. You're not going to be able to be effective. In fact, you probably won't open that account or develop the account, and you won't be successful in your career. You have to believe in yourself.

I've been involved in consulting many salespeople who at one point had a crisis of belief based on their own performance or something that happened within their company. Before I allowed them to say…

Oh, it's the company I work for.

It's the industry.

It's the geography.

It's the time we're in.

It's where I live.

It's the way I look.

I always said, "Look inside yourself and say, 'Do I believe in what I'm selling? Would I buy this product if I were a consumer? Would I buy from me? Would I buy from my company?'"

If you have true belief in yourself and your company, you can be unstoppable. Believe in you.

Get Excited

The third component of motivation is enthusiasm, being excited about what you're doing. In fact, let's demonstrate how it sounds when we're not excited. Slouch in your chair right now. Now say something and you can tell that your voice is different. You're just not as enthusiastic. Even though others can't see you, they can hear that your voice sounds differently when you're not excited.

Now sit up in your chair. You've only made that one change in your behavior. Speak again. Can you hear the difference in your voice and how enthusiastic your voice sounds now compared to when you were slouching?

If you're going through life depressed or unhappy—you don't know where your next mortgage payment's going to come from, you just had a fight with your spouse, or your boss tells you you're not making your numbers—and you approach your business with that state of mind, you are absolutely going to fail. If, on the other hand, you can apply the lesson that I'm about to share with you, you can overcome this mental state of not being excited.

Do you remember Pete Rose the major league baseball player? They called him Charlie Hustle. He wasn't the fastest, and he didn't have the most talent, yet he played the game with a zest, enjoyment, and enthusiasm that was contagious. When he hit the ball he sprinted down that first base line. Even if he had to slide headlong into first base, he'd do whatever he could to get on base safely. He was minor league in terms of ability, but he was a star in the major leagues.

Why? He was the most excitable, enthusiastic guy on the team. If someone had to slide in hard to break up a double play, it was Pete Rose. If someone had to run to the outfield to catch a pop fly, it was Rose. If someone had to bunt to get the runner to second base, it was him. He did everything he possibly could to help his team. Even when he wasn't playing, he was cheering; he was in the dugout being excited.

You know what he knew? He knew that if he was enthusiastic, it would help him be successful. Try it. It works.

Be Persistent

The fourth component of motivation is to be persistent. I had a very good client when I was in the office equipment business who was fabulously wealthy and successful. I said, "What's the secret to your success?"

He replied, "A lot of people knock on the door once, and if nobody answers they walk away. Or, if they get the wrong answer the first time, they walk away. I'm that guy who always keeps knocking on the door. If I can't get through that door, I'll try a different door. Or I'll go through the window, or around the block. I'll come through the roof. I'll do whatever it takes to get that face-to-face meeting or get that business." This means that if you practice persistence, if you are willing to come back over and over and over again without ever being a pest, you will be successful.

Yet persistence is usually the one inspiration that salespeople have the least amount of comfort with. It's been one of the techniques that I've used over the years to be quite successful in my career.

I was thinking about this the other day. I'm working with two really good clients who I'm having a hard time connecting with these days. They're busy; I'm busy. As I leave voice mails, send them emails, and tell them I'm going to follow up, I always wonder if my client base, or anybody's client base for that matter, ever is concerned about when salespeople cross the line from being a persistent person, which is good, to being a pest, which is bad.

What do you think is the most number of times I ever called a prospect before I got the appointment to get the business? If you guess ten, that would be a good guess, but it would be wrong. It's thirty-seven.

I had identified a key potential client. In fact, I had two referrals into this particular client. I was the person who taught the stockbrokers that helped bring this company public how to sell the offering successfully. I knew the story, I knew what was important to this company, and I had heard about the reputation of the president and CEO—that he was hard-working, dedicated, had a lot of irons in the fire, and was a committed, enthusiastic guy. That was one referral into that company.

The second referral is that the person I bought life insurance from also sold life insurance to this guy. And the life insurance person that I bought from was also someone that I taught the principles of Total Selling, and had attained a very high level of success with a very well known insurance company. So that was a second referral into this company.

I called him, left a voice mail, and he didn't call me back. I waited a week, I called him again; I waited a week, I called him again; I waited three days, I called him again. Each time I had something fresh to say on the phone. I waited three weeks; I called him again. I called him back in a week. I waited again. I called him again. I waited again. I called him again. And I kept track of all my calls. He hadn't returned thirty-seven of my phone calls over a seven-month period.

On the thirty-eighth dial, I was leaving one of my customized messages. "Hi Greg, this is Warren Wechsler with Total Selling. As you know, I'm the person who taught and inspired all the stockbrokers to work with their clients to bring your company public years ago. I also coach Mark Smith, who is your insurance agent, and is also my insurance agent.

I'm about to begin my fourth sentence in leaving my voice mail, and he picks up the phone. "Hello, Warren?" he says.

I said, "Yes?" I was stunned because I had left all those voice mails and not ever had one returned.

He said, "What are you doing next Thursday at two o'clock?" I said, "I'm meeting with you next Thursday at two o'clock, Greg!" And he replied, "That's right." It's a good thing I didn't say I had no idea, right?

Anyway, I showed up in a large conference room on Thursday. There were ten people around the table. Greg said, "This is my VP of technical support. This is my VP of sales. This is my VP of marketing. Here's my CFO." And so on.

Greg is sitting at the other end of the table with a door behind him, and I'm way at the other end of the table where they had saved a seat for me. Imagine I'm at one end of the table. He's at the other end of the table. I've never met this guy, and only left five hundred million voice mails for him. Along the sides of the table are all these very important people from his company.

He stands up after he makes the introduction. He looks at me, he looks at them, and says, "As long as Warren does everything that he's told me on the phone and that I've shared briefly with you—you've all seen his materials that I've handed around to you—and as long as what he talks about is within the budget that we agreed on before he stepped into the room, do whatever he says."

Then he got up, turned around, left the room, and closed the door behind him. The rest, shall we say, is history. I got the order on the spot after about two hours of discussions. After a year and a half of working with them, I kept calling Greg back to keep him informed about how well we were doing. He never returned another voice mail.

The moral of the story is not "isn't Warren great" because I'm not. I'm just an ordinary person who sometimes does extraordinary things, which is what salespeople do. But I'm telling you that story because it amplifies that if we are persistent in our efforts, and we never cross the line to become a pest, then it's good to be that type of person that pursues things to their proper end, especially if you have a strong belief that you can help these people, that you can be of service to them.

Be Proactive

The fifth component of motivation is to be proactive. The key is: there's a time to plan, and then it's time to act." So many of us go through life and we say, "Ready, ready, ready, ready. Aim, aim, aim, aim. Ready, ready. Aim, aim."

We never fire. We never pull the trigger. We never shoot the arrow. All the previous ideas about a sense of purpose and believing in you, being enthusiastic, and being persistent mean nothing unless you're willing to be proactive and take action.

If you add action to those other ideas, you will be successful. You will be self-motivated and inspired. And you know what else? You will be *inspiring*.

Other people will look up to you and they will attach themselves to you. They will be your fans. They will be your admirers.

Tomorrow Is Today

You may say, "Tomorrow I'm going to find a better job," "Tomorrow I'm going on a diet," "Tomorrow I'm going to start exercising," or, "Tomorrow I'm going to make five calls." You may have all these great ideas about "tomorrow, tomorrow, tomorrow," and you may feel great about yourself, but it's all a false feeling.

What happens is that you wake up the next morning and the first thing your brain says is "Is today tomorrow?" and the brain says, "No, today is today." Then your brain gives a big sigh of relief and says, "Oh great, because I'm going to start that project, I'm going to get that job, I'm going to be better, I'm going to eat healthier, I'm going to exercise more tomorrow." Today is not tomorrow so, alright, I'm off the hook.

The point is that tomorrow never comes. You have to live today. There is a whole series of today's—right now. You can't live your life in terms of tomorrow because "tomorrow" never comes.

Total Selling Toolkit

Total Selling Strategic Sales Plan

Your Company Name

_____

Salesperson

_____

Date_____

Dear Total Salesperson:

Thank you for taking the time to focus on your 200_ Total Selling Strategic Sales Plan. We all know that planning is an essential practice to accomplish meaningful goals. This is a tool which will help you in the following areas:

(1.) List your 200_ goals for maintaining and growing your business.

(2.) Help identify your current position with your "A" accounts.

(3.) Develop plans for "Building the Business" within your existing accounts.

(4.) Identify and develop a "Key Account Plan."

(5.) Conduct specific "Account Planning" for each of your "A" and "B" prospect and client accounts.

(6.) Create a review process to measure the progress towards your goals and ensure the success of your plan.

By doing the above six steps, you are creating an environment in which you will continue to be successful, grow and prosper.

Sincerely,

_____

Warren Wechsler

Business Gap Analysis

a. Current year actual sales: _____

b. Avg. % old business lost per year* _____

c. Next year sales projection if
   nothing changes (a - b) _____

d. Desired next year sales %
   increase in $ ___ (add to c) _____

e. Gap (d - c) _____

f. Current client annual % sales
   growth* in $ _____

g. Gap with current client growth
   factored in (e-f) _____

h. Average sale per new client* _____

i. New accounts needed to
   cover the gap _____

*If you don't have these actual numbers take your best educated guess, based on your experience with your clients. These are important numbers to track in the future!

Personal Sales Plan

1) Your Current Year Sales Volume:
   $_____

2) Your Next Year Sales Goal:
   $_____

SALES by Product / Service category

1) Your Current Year Product 1 Volume:
   $_____
   Your Next Year Product 1 Goal:
   $_____

2) Your Current Year Product 2 Volume
   $_____
   Your Next Year Product 2 Goal:
   $_____

3) Your Current Year Product 3 Volume:
   $_____
   Your Next Year Product 3 Goal:
   $_____

4) Your Current Year Product 4 Volume:
   $_____
   Your Next Year Product 4 Goal:
   $_____

5) Your Current Year Product 5 Volume:
   $_____
   Your Next Year Product 5 Goal:
   $_____

My Current Position with "A" Accounts

1) List up to ten (10) of your "A" customers

2) Rate each customer using the following system:

1 We are the Dominant Supplier (receiving 80% of the potential business)

2 We are an Above Average Supplier (receiving 50% or more of the potential)

3 We are a Below Average Supplier (receiving less than 50% of the potential)

4 We are not currently a Supplier (receiving 0% of the potential)

5 Not Applicable (this customer does not utilize this product or service category)

Customer 1 _____

Customer 2 _____

Customer 3 _____

	Rating	Rating	Rating
Product 1	_____	_____	_____
Product 2	_____	_____	_____
Product 3	_____	_____	_____
Product 4	_____	_____	_____
Product 5	_____	_____	_____

Sales strategy for "A" and "B" Customers (retention, growth, referral)

Account 1

_____Rating_____

Potential Sales Strategy

_____

Account 2

_____Rating_____

Potential Sales Strategy_____

_____

Account 3

_____Rating_____

Potential Sales Strategy_____

_____

Account 4

_____Rating_____

Potential Sales Strategy_____

_____

Account 5

_____Rating_____

Potential Sales Strategy_____

_____

Building Business With Existing Clients

Plans for increasing business from existing "A" accounts:

_____

_____

_____

Plans for increasing business from "C" accounts with "A" or "B" potential:_____

_____

_____

_____

_____

Plans for maintaining customer *relationships* that I now have:

_____

_____

_____

_____

Key Account Planning

Salesperson _____Location_____Date_____

Account_____Rating (A-B-C)_____

Phone Number_____Fax_____email_____

Address_____City_____

State_____Zip_____

Product	Current Year $	Next Year Potential $	Next Year Service Actual $
1. _____	_____	_____	_____
2. _____	_____	_____	_____
3. _____	_____	_____	_____
4. _____	_____	_____	_____
5. _____	_____	_____	_____

Decision Maker
(Need)_____Title_____
Decision Maker
(Authority)_____Title_____
Decision Maker
(Money)_____Title_____
Decision Influencer
(Champion)_____Title_____
Administrative Asst._____
Competitors:_____
Similar customers that buy from us:_____

_____

Key Account Planning—Action Plan:

Appointment Approach (referral, rationale, benefit to the customer):

_____

_____

_____

Positioning of our company vs. the competition:

_____

_____

Key questions to ask this account:

_____

_____

_____

Potential resistance and my response:

_____

_____

Tactics for maintaining the initiative and next steps:

_____

_____

_____

_____

_____

_____

Top Ten Advocate System Worksheet
For the month of _____ Year _____

Name Company Title Relationship Type of Contact

1.

2.

3.

4.

5.

6.

7.

8.

9.

10.

Best prospects

My ten best prospect accounts (by industry, revenue size, employee size, geography, etc.)

1.

2.

3.

4.

5.

6.

7.

8.

9.

10.

Coaching Session Planning Guide

Coach:_____ Salesperson:_____ Date:_____

Business Analysis:

Sales results this period:_____

+/- % to goal:_____

Current account$_____Current account growth $_____

New account $_____

# of initial approaches this period:_____

# of appointments booked this period:_____

new accounts this period:_____

Activity Evaluation:

What worked this week? Why?

_____

_____

What didn't work this week? Why?

_____

_____

Other factors:

_____

_____

Action Steps:

What's the next opportunity?

_____

Action plan (specific, behavioral activities!)

_____

_____

_____

Resources: What do I need to learn/find? Who can help me?

_____

_____

Top 3 priorities: *These are your accountabilities for the next coaching session.*

1.

2.

3.

Salesperson / Manager Quarterly Review

Date_____

Current Quarter Results	Actual	Projected Difference
Overall_____	_____	_____
Product 1_____	_____	_____
Product 2_____	_____	_____
Product 3_____	_____	_____
Profitability_____	_____	_____

Discussion
Items:_____
_____
_____
_____
_____

Conclusions and Follow-up plans:
_____
_____
_____
_____
_____
_____

Salesperson _____
Manager _____

Self Behavioral Observations

<u>Strengths</u>   <u>Opportunities</u>

Identifying
Prospects

Finding Decision
Maker Criteria

Arrange Initial
Appointments

Asking the
Right Questions

Presenting
Solutions

Asking for
Commitments

Action Steps based on changes desired:
1.
2.
3.
4.
5.

Key Priorities for this period's personal development:
1.
2.

Index

About the Author

Warren Wechsler is founder and president of Total Selling, Inc. He is an acknowledged expert in the world of business-to-business selling and is well known as a leading international sales resource to sales people, sales executives, and sales organizations.

Warren works with sales people who are committed to excellence in selling and with business executives and sales leaders who demand superior performance. He is heard weekly on his syndicated radio show, "Total Selling with Warren Wechsler", and his website, www.totalselling.com, is recognized as a premier destination by many of the finest companies in the world, whose sales educators are frequent visitors to the site to download information for use by their sales people worldwide.

Clients include Fortune 500 companies, INC. 500 companies and hundreds of other companies in a wide variety of industries, including financial services, manufacturing, banking, insurance, distribution and professional services. Warren delivers keynote presentations, presents seminars, and leads workshops to teach people the selling, planning, and organizing skills that are essential to their sales success. He shares tools and techniques for professional selling that inspire sales people to expand their sales and enhance their career satisfaction—and enjoy the journey.

Contact Warren Wechsler at warren@totalselling.com.